D1624932

a SAVOR THE SOUTH® *cookbook*

Southern Holidays

SAVOR THE SOUTH® *cookbooks*

Southern Holidays, by Debbie Moose (2014)

Sweet Potatoes, by April McGreger (2014)

Okra, by Virginia Willis (2014)

Pickles and Preserves, by Andrea Weigl (2014)

Bourbon, by Kathleen Purvis (2013)

Biscuits, by Belinda Ellis (2013)

Tomatoes, by Miriam Rubin (2013)

Peaches, by Kelly Alexander (2013)

Pecans, by Kathleen Purvis (2012)

Buttermilk, by Debbie Moose (2012)

a SAVOR THE SOUTH® *cookbook*

Southern Holidays

DEBBIE MOOSE

The University of North Carolina Press CHAPEL HILL

The paper in this book meets the guidelines for permanence and durability of the Committee on Production Guidelines for Book Longevity of the Council on Library Resources. The University of North Carolina Press has been a member of the Green Press Initiative since 2003.

Jacket illustration: Coconut cake, © DebbiSmirnoff/iStockphoto; cake stand base, © allenmorrisphoto/iStockphoto; confetti, © BanksPhotos/iStockphoto.

Library of Congress Cataloging-in-Publication Data
Moose, Debbie.
Southern holidays : a savor the South cookbook / Debbie Moose.
pages cm   Includes index.
ISBN 978-1-4696-1789-3 (cloth : alk. paper)
ISBN 978-1-4696-1790-9 (ebook)
1. Cooking, American—Southern style. 2. Holiday cooking.
3. Seasonal cooking. I. Title.
TX715.2.S68M6645 2014   641.5975—dc23   2014012922

18 17 16 15 14   5 4 3 2 1

Sweet Potatoes Restaurant's Quick and Easy Hoppin' John Soup is reprinted with permission from Stephanie L. Tyson, *Well, Shut My Mouth! The Sweet Potatoes Restaurant Cookbook* (Winston-Salem, NC: John F. Blair, 2011); How to Do Your Own Oyster Roast is reprinted from Elizabeth Wiegand, *The Outer Banks Cookbook: Recipes and Traditions from North Carolina's Barrier Islands*, © 2013 Morris Book Publishing, LLC, used by permission of the publisher, Globe Pequot Press; Nanticoke Catfish originally appeared in *The Chesapeake Bay through Ebony Eyes* and is reprinted with permission from Adrian Miller, *Soul Food: The Surprising Story of an American Cuisine, One Plate at a Time* (Chapel Hill: University of North Carolina Press, 2013).

To Rob

Did you really think I was going to stop

after five books?

Contents

INTRODUCTION For Southerners, Practically
Every Day's a Holiday 1

Winter 5
Special Treats from Christmas Coconut Cake to
St. Joseph's Day Cookies

HANUKKAH 7

Chipotle Brisket 8

Sweet Potato Latkes 10

CHRISTMAS EVE AND CHRISTMAS DAY 11

Martha's Chicken Pie 12

My Favorite Fruitcake 14

Holiday Coconut Cake 16

Moravian Sugar Cake 18

Lemon-Lavender Jelly 20

Café Brûlot 21

KWANZAA 22

Not Your Grandmother's Ambrosia 23

Peanut Butter Muffins with Chocolate Drizzle 24

NEW YEAR'S DAY 26

Apple and Bacon–Stuffed Collard Roll-Ups 27

Sweet Potatoes Restaurant's Quick and Easy
Hoppin' John Soup 28

OLD CHRISTMAS 30

Sassy Cocktail Sauce 31

How to Do Your Own Oyster Roast 32

MARDI GRAS 34

Brandy Milk Punch 35

Coconut King Cake 36

ST. JOSEPH'S DAY 38

Pasta Milanese with Mudrica 39

Cuccidati 41

MARCH MADNESS 43

Very Veggie Brunch Casserole 44

Smokin' Mary 45

Spring 47
There's Ham on the Easter Table, and Seafood Abounds
as Fleets Set Sail for the Season

BLESSING OF THE FLEET 48

Vietnamese Spring Rolls 49

Seafood Gumbo 51

PASSOVER 53

Matzoh Balls, Cajun Style 54

Sephardic Matzoh Lasagna 56

EASTER 58

Hop-into-Spring Deviled Eggs 59

Jeanne's Slow-Cooker Country Ham 60

Hot Cross Buns 62

Market Fresh Potato Salad 64

Summer 65
Southerners Celebrate Special Foods
and Moments in History

PEACH FESTIVALS 66

Peach and Prosciutto Salad 67

Creamy Peach Parfaits 68

Ginger-Peach Soda 70

JUNETEENTH 72

Smoky Red Rice 73

Nanticoke Catfish 74

Rosy Roselle Sipper 76

INDEPENDENCE DAY 77

Chef & the Farmer's Sugar Baby Watermelon Salad
with Jalapeño Vinaigrette 78

John's Great Greek Burger 80

Black Bean Summer Salad 82

Watermelon Lemonade 83

Fall 85

Thanksgiving Feasts and Ethnic Food Celebrations
Make the Season Glow

GREEK FESTIVAL 86

Greek Chicken 87

Loukoumades 89

SHALOM Y'ALL JEWISH FOOD FESTIVAL 91

Food Fest Blintzes 92

Chopped Liver Appetizer Spread 95

ShaLoMein 96

THANKSGIVING 98

Cajun-Style Rice Dressing 99

Carol's Sweet Potato Casserole 100

Aunt Ida's Turkey 102

Mrs. Rozar's Giblet Gravy 104

Apple Pie from the Sisters of Pie 105

Cranberry-Orange Pie 108

Sorghum Pecan Pie 109

Acknowledgments 110   *Index* 111

a SAVOR THE SOUTH® *cookbook*

Southern Holidays

Introduction

Southerners really know how to throw a party, and a holiday is the best excuse of all for one. We bring out our cherished family recipes, sprinkle in some new ideas, and start celebrating.

And we have a delightfully broad definition of "holiday."

We respect tradition, but we bring our special culinary touches to even the most traditional of holidays, such as Hanukkah, Christmas, Easter, and Thanksgiving.

But the regular calendar holidays aren't enough for us. We hold festivals for the sole purpose of celebrating beloved regional foods, such as peaches and seafood. We honor parts of history along with good things to eat, marking the contributions of African Americans, Italians, Greeks, Germans, Jews, and others to the gumbo that is today's southern culture. If you look at the South through its food, you'll realize the region has always been more diverse than people think, especially today.

And everyone knows that anything associated with college basketball is a holiday in these parts—don't even *try* to argue about that.

The food served at holiday events has both personal and cultural connections. Special dishes carry specific memories for each family, but many also have roots in a common past. You can trace them back like a golden thread that ties families together, no matter how different, in a shared southern history. The Thanksgiving sweet potato casserole is one example. Now it's on holiday tables from Seattle to St. Augustine, with or without little marshmallows on top, but it most likely got started in the South. This region has long been a prime area for growing sweet potatoes. North Carolina produces more of them than any other state, according to 2011 figures. We had them, so we used them. And, lo, the delectable sweet potato casserole spread across the land as southerners moved to other areas of the United States and cooking magazines popularized the recipes, according to historians at Plimoth Plantation, a living-history museum near the site of the *Mayflower's* seventeenth-century landing in Massachusetts. The South can also claim the first officially decreed Thanksgiving, long before the Pilgrims showed up, but more on that later.

Because we love sweets, southerners also expanded Thanksgiving desserts beyond stuffy old New England mincemeat and pumpkin pies. Today, such additions as the sweetly indulgent pecan pie are classics on tables around the country—although at my house, we love apple pie for reasons I'll explain below. Those are all desserts to be thankful for.

There's more. How about those glazed spiral-sliced hams that are stars of the show at Easter meals? Their place on that holiday's table goes back to farming days in the hog-centric South, and I'll tell you more about that in the pages that follow. So if you're enjoying a big slice of ham at Easter lunch in Milwaukee, we'll be glad to claim you, as long as you remember that what we call dinner is what you call lunch.

Also, there are historical reasons for the coconut cake's honored place on the Christmas dessert table that just make it taste even better.

I discovered fascinating holiday connections between the personal and the cultural while working on this book. When I was a kid in Winston-Salem, North Carolina, Christmas was the only time of year my mother purchased a particular dessert from a neighborhood dairy bar. It was called Flaming Snowballs and consisted of balls of hard-frozen vanilla ice cream rolled in coconut with a red candle and a bit of artificial holly in each one. After supper on Christmas Eve, we lit the candles and blew them out fast, before red wax could drip on the coconut—I didn't want to miss a shred of it. Another more puzzling habit of my mother's was to have Santa fill my stocking with oranges and tangerines, then perch some small gift on top. I always thought Santa was cheap. My friends got stockings full of toys rather than edibles,

and these were not even unusual edibles but food we could get year-round. Later, I found out that the snowballs and the fruit have a shared history as railroads helped spread exotic treats such as coconuts and citrus fruit from southern port cities across the region. However, at that time they were still expensive and rare and reserved for special occasions. For people like my mother, who grew up in a rural North Carolina town at the end of the Great Depression, oranges might be their only Christmas gift and a homemade coconut cake was a once-a-year event. The memories persisted for her, and even as an adult, her favorite Christmas present was a box of navel oranges.

Because the regular-old holidays aren't sufficient for southerners, we extend the celebrations to honor favorite foods and ethnic heritage. Across the region, you can find festivals in praise of collards, okra, shrimp, strawberries, peaches, shad (a kind of fish), watermelon, biscuits, ramps (wild onions), barbecue (of course), and many more foods. From Lebanese Americans in the Delta to Greek Americans in South Carolina, ethnic food festivals allow visitors to taste the world. And one of the oldest Jewish food festivals in the South, Shalom Y'all, takes place each year in Savannah, Georgia.

In this book, you'll find the recipes collected by holiday and the holidays grouped by season. I set the seasons by the dates of the equinoxes and solstices when they officially begin.

It's impossible to include every holiday favorite from every part of the South in one little cookbook like this. My goal is to offer a taste of the variety of celebrations across the region, featuring recipes cherished by real southerners. I hope you'll see this book as a collection of holiday greeting cards that remind you to enjoy and preserve your own treasured food traditions and help get you acquainted with some new ones. Like I did while writing the book, you might learn a few bits of history you didn't know.

Winter

SPECIAL TREATS FROM CHRISTMAS COCONUT CAKE TO ST. JOSEPH'S DAY COOKIES

The darkest season offers the brightest festivities. Try sizzling Hanukkah latkes with a southern twist or Moravian baked goods on Christmas morning. And basketball fans, lift a toast to your favorite team!

Hanukkah

DECEMBER

I didn't know any Jews when I was growing up in my white-bread-and-pork-chop world outside Winston-Salem, North Carolina.

When I married a Jewish man, he came with a new world of food, some of which required adjustment. Smoked whitefish with the head on for breakfast—I swear the eyes were staring at me—was a big one.

However, I cruised right into Hanukkah. Latkes are fried potato pancakes. Who doesn't love those? As a devoted new wife, I strived for hours to create grease-free latkes until my husband informed me that the grease is what they're all about since Hanukkah commemorates a miracle in which one day's worth of oil kept temple lamps burning for eight days.

Jews have long been part of the South after arriving in Savannah, Georgia, and Charleston, South Carolina, in the sixteenth and seventeenth centuries. The settlers, many of whom had fled the Spanish Inquisition, were seeking religious freedom. From 1776 to 1820, there were more Jews in Charleston than in any other American city, according to *Matzoh Ball Gumbo: Culinary Tales of the Jewish South* by Marcie Cohen Ferris.

Chipotle Brisket

I always thought my husband's family was afraid to let us host Jewish holiday meals because they suspected I would do something like sneak jalapeños into the gefilte fish (which would improve the stuff, in my view). Well, this is not your Bubbe's brisket, but everyone likes it. Be sure to get the thicker point cut of the brisket. This goes in the slow-cooker, so it's super easy.

MAKES 4–6 SERVINGS

FOR THE RUB

2 tablespoons paprika (regular or smoked or a combination)
1 tablespoon black pepper
1½ teaspoons salt
1 tablespoon garlic powder
1 tablespoon chili powder
¼ teaspoon cayenne pepper
1 tablespoon brown sugar

FOR THE BRISKET

1 (4- to 5-pound) beef brisket, point cut, trimmed of excess fat
¾ cup brown sugar, divided
¼ cup plus 2 tablespoons Worcestershire sauce, divided
2 tablespoons balsamic vinegar
1 (14-ounce) can diced tomatoes
¼ cup maple syrup
3 large chipotle peppers in adobo sauce, chopped,
    plus 1 tablespoon adobo sauce
¼ cup white wine vinegar
¼ cup orange juice
1 heaping teaspoon garlic powder
1 tablespoon dry mustard
1 teaspoon salt
1 teaspoon black pepper

To make the rub, in a small bowl, combine the paprika, black pepper, salt, garlic powder, chili powder, cayenne pepper, and brown sugar. Rub the mixture on both sides of the brisket and place in a shallow baking dish.

Stir ½ cup of the brown sugar, ¼ cup of the Worcestershire sauce, and the balsamic vinegar together in a small bowl and pour it over the brisket. Turn to coat both sides, then cover and refrigerate overnight.

In a saucepan, combine the tomatoes, maple syrup, chipotle peppers, adobo sauce, white wine vinegar, orange juice, garlic powder, dry mustard, salt, and pepper and the remaining ¼ cup brown sugar and 2 tablespoons Worcestershire sauce. Bring to a boil, reduce the heat, and simmer for about 20 minutes or until reduced by a third. Cover and refrigerate. This sauce can be made up to 1 day ahead.

When ready to cook, put the brisket in a slow cooker. Pour about two-thirds of the sauce over the brisket. Cover and cook on low heat for 5–6 hours or until the meat is tender. Warm the remaining sauce to serve with the brisket.

Sweet Potato Latkes

I didn't know a thing about latkes when I married my husband, so when I started cooking them, of course I had to tweak tradition. I came up with this version, using one of my favorite southern vegetables and a little spice, which is our favorite today. I save time and grate the sweet potatoes and onion together in a food processor.

MAKES 4 SERVINGS

2 cups coarsely grated sweet potatoes
1 small onion, coarsely grated
2 large eggs, lightly beaten
2 tablespoons flour
1 teaspoon salt
1 teaspoon chili powder
½ teaspoon cinnamon
Vegetable oil
Applesauce and sour cream

In a large bowl, combine the sweet potatoes, onion, eggs, flour, salt, chili powder, and cinnamon. Heat about 1 inch of vegetable oil in a large frying pan over medium heat.

Scoop out about 2 tablespoons of the sweet potato mixture per latke and place in the hot oil. Don't crowd the pan so the oil will stay hot. Press the patties gently with the back of a spoon to flatten them out. Fry, turning once, until browned on both sides.

Drain on a wire rack placed over a platter for a few minutes, then transfer to a paper towel–lined platter and keep warm in the oven while you fry the remaining latkes. Serve with applesauce and sour cream.

Christmas Eve and Christmas Day

DECEMBER 24 AND 25

My husband and I stayed in a Key West bed and breakfast one Christmas week that was bedecked with more "Let it snow" signs than icicles in Minnesota, showing that southerners don't let reality stand in the way of the party at Christmastime.

And partytime it is. Communities and families burnish cherished traditions and create new ones. In Cajun country, bonfires along Mississippi levees light the way for Santa Claus. Christmas parades in coastal communities feature boats instead of floats.

December brings a monthlong feast. Pig roasts in Florida's Cuban community. Oyster roasts on the Carolina coasts. Festive beverages for toasting the season in New Orleans. And sweets everywhere. This time of year, southern cooks step up their games, bringing out their best cakes, pies, and cookies.

My childhood Christmas memory: A coconut cake sitting on a card table in the center of an otherwise empty screened porch. My grandmother in Statesville, North Carolina, used the chilly porch as extra storage space because her refrigerator was packed with the rest of the Christmas feast that she single-handedly prepared. The cake was the star, waiting in its private green room until time for it to make a grand entrance.

Martha's Chicken Pie

This recipe from my friend Martha Waggoner is a Christmas Eve tradition at her house. The recipe is more than thirty years old, and she thinks it may have originated in a newspaper. She grew up in Winston-Salem, North Carolina, where Moravian-style pies like this one—all meat, no vegetables—are popular. Martha serves it with baked apples and a simple vegetable.

MAKES 2 PIES

- 4¼ cups plus 1 tablespoon flour, divided
- 1¾ cups vegetable shortening
- 1 tablespoon sugar
- 2 teaspoons salt, plus more to taste
- 1 tablespoon vinegar
- 1 large egg
- 3½–4 pounds bone-in chicken breasts
- Black pepper
- 4 tablespoons unsalted butter, divided
- 1 cup milk
- 1 cup chicken broth

In a large bowl, use a pastry blender to combine 4 cups of the flour with the shortening, sugar, and salt until the mixture resembles small peas. In a separate small bowl, beat together the vinegar, the egg, and ½ cup cold tap water. Stir the vinegar mixture into the flour mixture until the flour is moistened. Use your hands to mold the dough into 2 balls, then wrap the balls in waxed paper and refrigerate for at least 15 minutes or up to 3 days.

Place the chicken in a large stockpot or Dutch oven and cover with water. Bring to a boil, then reduce the heat to a simmer and cook until the chicken is tender and cooked through, 20–30 minutes, depending on the sizes of the pieces. Remove the chicken and let it cool until you can handle it. Remove the meat from the bones, discarding the bones and skin, and chop it. Reserve 1 cup of the broth from cooking the chicken.

To prepare the pies, preheat the oven to 400°. Remove 1 dough ball from the refrigerator and cut it in half. On a well-floured surface with a well-floured rolling pin, roll out one half so it fits into a 9-inch pie pan. Place half of the chicken in the bottom crust and add salt and pepper to taste. Repeat the process with the second dough ball. You will have 2 (9-inch) pies.

In a saucepan over medium heat, melt 3 tablespoons of the butter. Stir in 1 tablespoon of the flour, then the milk and chicken broth. Cook, stirring, until the mixture is slightly thickened. Divide the mixture between the two pies, pouring it over the chicken.

Divide the remaining dough ball in half and roll out two top crusts. Place them over the chicken and press along the edge of the pans with a fork to seal the crusts. With a sharp knife, cut 4 slashes in each top crust to vent. Melt the remaining 1 tablespoon butter and stir in the remaining ¼ cup flour. Sprinkle the mixture evenly over the top crusts of the pies.

Place the pies on a rimmed baking sheet to catch any leaks. Bake for 20 minutes or until browned.

NOTE ✳ The pies can be made ahead and frozen before adding the butter-flour topping and baking. Seal them in freezer bags. To cook, thaw overnight in the refrigerator, then add the butter-flour topping and bake.

My Favorite Fruitcake

I love fruitcake, and I don't care who knows it. I spent many years coming up with this version, which uses dried fruit instead of candied fruit. Maybe that's why it appeals even to fruitcake haters. Or maybe it's the rum. Either way, if Truman Capote can write the lovely "A Christmas Memory," which features making fruitcake as its central event, I feel no qualms about placing this cake on my holiday table.

MAKES 2 FRUITCAKES

3 cups chopped dried fruit (I like mango, pineapple, and apricot)

1 cup golden raisins

Dark rum

4 cups flour, divided

1 teaspoon baking powder

½ teaspoon salt

12 tablespoons unsalted butter, at room temperature

2 cups sugar

5 large eggs

1 teaspoon vanilla

1 cup chopped pecans

Put the dried fruit and raisins in a large bowl and add enough rum to cover the fruit completely. Let it sit for 30 minutes, then drain the fruit well and toss it with ½ cup of the flour.

Preheat the oven to 350°. Spray 2 (9 × 5-inch) loaf pans with nonstick cooking spray and set aside.

Sift the remaining 3½ cups flour together with the baking powder and salt in a small bowl.

Place the butter and sugar in the bowl of a stand mixer fitted with the paddle blade and cream until light and fluffy. Add the eggs one at a time, mixing well after each. Beat in the vanilla.

Beat the flour mixture into the butter mixture, beginning with the mixer on low and increasing the speed to medium as the flour is incorporated, until the batter is smooth. Scrape the sides of the bowl with a spatula to be sure all is combined. Either with a large spatula or with the mixer on the lowest setting, gently stir in the fruit and pecans. The batter will be very thick and heavy. Pour the batter evenly into the 2 prepared loaf pans. Bake for about 1 hour or until the cakes test done. Place the pans on wire racks until they are no longer hot to the touch, then remove the cakes and cool completely on the racks.

Optional but good: After the cakes have been removed from the pans and are completely cool, soak cheesecloth in rum and wrap each cake in it. Then wrap the cakes in aluminum foil (to help keep the cheesecloth on) and place them in a reclosable plastic bag. Let sit at room temperature for 2–3 days for the rum to soak in. At that point, soak the cloth again and replace it as you eat the cakes.

Holiday Coconut Cake

Even more than fruitcake, coconut cake is a southern Christmas tradition. By the nineteenth century, railroads transported special treats once found only in port cities to towns all over the South, and coconut was one that arrived in December. The work involved in cracking and grating the coconut also made coconut cake a special-occasion dessert. And the seven-minute frosting traditionally used can flop into a grainy mess on humid days, which abound until late fall, so winter was the ideal time to make the cake. After I burned out a mixer and spent hours turning out a gluey mass of frosting, I came up with this easier version. It's not the same as my grandmother's, but it's still beautiful and delicious.

MAKES 10 SERVINGS

- 2 cups sifted cake flour
- 2 teaspoons baking powder
- 1/4 teaspoon salt
- 3 large eggs, separated
- 10 tablespoons unsalted butter, at room temperature
- 3 cups sugar, divided
- 2/3 cup canned coconut milk, well shaken
  (not reduced-fat or fat-free)
- 2 teaspoons vanilla, divided
- 2 cups sour cream (not reduced-fat or fat-free)
- 2 1/2 cups flaked, sweetened frozen coconut, thawed but
  still cold, divided

Preheat the oven to 350°. Butter and flour 2 (9-inch) cake pans.

In a small bowl, sift together the flour, baking powder, and salt.

Place the egg whites in a clean, dry bowl and beat them with an electric mixer until they're stiff but not dry.

In another clean bowl, using an electric mixer with clean beaters, cream the butter and 1½ cups of the sugar until light and fluffy. Add the egg yolks and beat well. Combine the coconut milk and 1 teaspoon of the vanilla in a small bowl and stir into the yolk mixture alternately with the flour mixture until fully combined. Using a spatula, fold in a third of the egg whites, then gently fold in the remaining egg whites. Don't overmix.

Divide the batter evenly between the 2 prepared pans and bake for 25 minutes or until a toothpick inserted in the center of each layer comes out clean. Cool the cakes in the pans for 10 minutes, then turn them out onto wire racks to cool completely.

While the cakes are cooling, prepare the frosting. In a medium bowl, stir together the remaining 1½ cups sugar and 1 teaspoon vanilla, the sour cream, and 2¼ cups of the coconut. Refrigerate for 30 minutes.

To prepare the cake, slice both layers horizontally with a long serrated bread knife to create 4 layers. Place 1 layer, cut side up, on a serving plate. Using a wooden skewer, carefully poke several holes completely through the layer. Poke straight down and pull straight up to avoid tearing the cake. Spread about one-quarter of the frosting on the bottom layer. Repeat with 2 more layers. Place the top layer cut-side down and do not poke holes in it. Spread the remaining frosting on the top only (not on the sides), then sprinkle the top with the remaining ¼ cup coconut.

Cover the cake and refrigerate it for at least 2 hours but preferably overnight. Serve straight from the refrigerator and refrigerate any leftovers.

Moravian Sugar Cake

Winston-Salem, North Carolina, has a Moravian community that goes back to the 1700s, when members of the church founded Old Salem. Moravian breads, which come from the German baking tradition, are wonderful, and this sweet yeasted coffee cake was a holiday favorite of mine growing up. Today, I follow the lead of my neighbor, Cathy Hedburg, who bakes and freezes sugar cakes in disposable foil pans for Christmas gifts. They're great for breakfast on Christmas Day.

MAKES 3 SUGAR CAKES

FOR THE CAKE
2 (¼-ounce) packages active dry yeast

⅔ cup plain, unseasoned mashed potatoes (see Note)

1 stick unsalted butter, at room temperature

¼ cup vegetable shortening

1 cup sugar

2 teaspoons salt

2 large eggs, slightly beaten

3½–4 cups flour

FOR THE TOPPING
¾ cup brown sugar

3 teaspoons cinnamon

1 stick unsalted butter, melted and slightly cooled

Preheat the oven to 375°. Butter 3 (9-inch) cake pans.

In a small bowl, dissolve the yeast in ½ cup warm water. Set aside until it foams, about 10 minutes.

In the bowl of a stand mixer, combine the mashed potatoes, 1 cup hot tap water, and the butter, shortening, sugar, and salt. Mix on low until the ingredients look like watery scrambled eggs. Stir in the eggs and dissolved yeast. Gradually stir in the flour until the dough resembles a heavy but not too dry muffin batter. Cover the bowl with a lint-free tea towel and let the dough rise in a warm place until doubled in size, about 1½ hours.

Punch down the dough, then divide it evenly among the 3 prepared cake pans. Cover the pans with your trusty tea towel and let the dough in each pan rise in a warm place until it reaches the top of the pan, about 30 minutes.

Prepare the topping by stirring together the brown sugar, cinnamon, and melted butter until combined.

Use your thumb to make indentations all over the top of the dough in each pan, about 1 inch apart. Push all the way to the bottom of each pan. Drizzle the topping evenly over the 3 cakes.

Bake for 15–20 minutes or until light brown. Serve warm or cool completely, place in airtight plastic freezer bags, and freeze.

NOTE ✳ If using leftover mashed potatoes, be sure they contain no butter, milk, or salt. You can use instant mashed potatoes, but be sure to buy the unseasoned variety.

Lemon-Lavender Jelly

Two friends and I spend summers making jams, jellies, pickles, and relishes from fresh fruits and vegetables. I give most of mine away as Christmas gifts. One December, I opened my box of goodies, ready to pack gifts, and discovered that a batch of plum jelly had failed to jell. To fill the shortage, I came up with this unusual jelly that can be made any time of year. My friends liked the flavor, and now it's a rightful member of the holiday team.

MAKES 4 HALF-PINT JARS

Zest of 1 large lemon, coarsely chopped
1 teaspoon dried lavender (see Note)
3½ cups sugar
¼ cup distilled white vinegar
1 tablespoon fresh lemon juice
1 (3-ounce) pouch liquid pectin

Place the lemon zest and lavender in a large bowl, pour 2¼ cups boiling water over them, cover, and let sit for 1 hour. Strain the liquid into a large saucepan, discarding the solids.

Add the sugar, vinegar, and lemon juice to the lemon zest–lavender liquid. Bring the mixture to a rolling boil over high heat, stirring constantly to dissolve the sugar. When it comes to a boil, stir in the pectin and return to a boil. Boil hard for 1–2 minutes, stirring occasionally, until the liquid thickens and drops in a loose sheet from a spoon.

Remove the saucepan from the heat and ladle the mixture into sterilized half-pint jars. Screw on sterilized lids. Process the jars in a boiling-water-bath canner for 5 minutes, then remove from the canner and let cool on folded kitchen towels or cooling racks. Do not disturb the jars for 24 hours to be sure they seal properly.

NOTE ❋ Be sure to use dried lavender labeled for culinary use that has not been sprayed with chemicals.

Café Brûlot

This isn't just a cocktail; it's an event. I adapted the recipe from one provided by Liz Williams of the Southern Food and Beverage Museum in New Orleans, who said it's a popular celebratory beverage during the holidays. My tester said if you want to make a real show of it for your guests, place the hot coffee in a pot on a heatproof trivet and the cups nearby on a tray. Place the spiced brandy or bourbon in a chafing dish (or in a heatproof bowl if you heat it on the stove) next to the tray and ignite the liquid, then add the coffee to it and pour it into the cups. If the flame goes out, you'll lose the show but still have a great-tasting cocktail.

MAKES 8 DRINKS

8 sugar cubes
Zest of 1 orange and 1 lemon, without pith,
   in large pieces
1 small cinnamon stick
¼ teaspoon whole cloves
½ cup brandy or bourbon
3 cups hot, freshly brewed dark-roast coffee,
   preferably with chicory

Rub the sugar cubes with the orange and lemon zest. Discard the zest. Place 1 sugar cube in each of the demitasse- or espresso-size (about 3-ounce) cups.

Combine the cinnamon stick, cloves, and brandy or bourbon in a chafing dish and gently warm the mixture for a few minutes or warm it in a saucepan on the stove over low heat. Use a long-handled match or lighter to ignite the mixture. Quickly stir in the coffee, then ladle the drink into the cups while still burning. Stir before drinking to dissolve the sugar cubes.

Kwanzaa

This holiday, which was created in California in the mid-1960s as an outgrowth of black nationalist movements, has evolved into a celebration of community, African history, and diversity. It's not a religious holiday, and plenty of people observe Christmas or Hanukkah along with Kwanzaa.

The multicultural aspects of the holiday are evident at celebrations such as the one the city of Durham, North Carolina, has sponsored for more than twenty-five years. The event draws people of various backgrounds from inside and outside the African American community for storytelling, dancing, and craft exhibits.

Each of the seven days of Kwanzaa focuses on a different principle: unity, self-determination, responsibility for others, cooperative economics, purpose, creativity, and faith. A candle is lit on each of the seven days, and symbolic foods are displayed.

According to African American food historian Michael W. Twitty, many ingredients important in southern cooking are traditional elements of African cuisines, including hot peppers, tomatoes, okra, black-eyed peas, peanuts, and watermelons. Bananas, mangoes, and coconuts came to Africa from Asia, then made their way to the New World. And the name "Kwanzaa" comes from a Swahili word that means "the first fruits of the harvest."

Not Your Grandmother's Ambrosia

Many southerners remember that big bowl of fruit on holiday tables—often canned, frosty with coconut, studded with mini-marshmallows, and laden with candy-sweet red maraschino cherries. But ambrosia has an honorable history, with recipes going back to the late 1800s. I came up with a less sweet version that can be a side dish or a light dessert.

MAKES 8 SERVINGS

4 cups fresh orange sections, white pith removed
1½ cups grated coconut (fresh or frozen and thawed)
2 cups fresh pineapple chunks
4 teaspoons confectioners' sugar, or to taste (see Note)
⅓ cup coconut water (see Note)
6 red maraschino cherries

Layer this salad in a tall glass bowl or trifle bowl as follows: 2 cups of the orange sections, ½ cup of the coconut, all the pineapple chunks, 2 teaspoons of the confectioners' sugar, ½ cup of the coconut, the remaining 2 cups orange sections, the remaining ½ cup coconut, and the remaining 2 teaspoons confectioners' sugar.

Gently pour the coconut water over the top, letting it moisten all the layers of fruit. Garnish with the maraschino cherries. Cover the bowl with plastic wrap and refrigerate for at least 2 hours or up to 8 hours.

NOTE ❋ A small amount of sugar helps release the juices in the fruit. The amount you use depends on how sweet your fruit is and your personal preference. Taste some of the fruit you're using and decide if you want more sugar, but this should not be an extremely sweet dish. Coconut water is a new product found in supermarket juice aisles. If you can't find coconut water, you can substitute orange juice, but do not use coconut milk.

Peanut Butter Muffins with Chocolate Drizzle

Dishes using peanuts or peanut butter are traditional at Kwanzaa because peanuts are a staple of African cooking. The nickname "goober" for peanuts comes from an African word for the legume. These muffins went fast among my taster's kids—she had to fight them off to get one. Natural peanut butter is the kind where the oil must be stirred back in before using. It gives more peanut flavor and texture to the muffins than conventional peanut butter.

MAKES 12 MUFFINS

- 2 cups flour
- 1 cup packed brown sugar
- 1 teaspoon salt
- 2 teaspoons baking powder
- 1 cup crunchy natural peanut butter, well stirred
- 1 cup milk
- 1 large egg
- ½ teaspoon vanilla
- 2 tablespoons unsalted butter, melted and slightly cooled
- 2 ounces bittersweet chocolate, melted

Preheat the oven to 350°. Spray a muffin pan with nonstick cooking spray.

In a large bowl, combine the flour and brown sugar. Use a whisk to break up any chunks of brown sugar and mix the brown sugar into the flour. Add the salt and baking powder and whisk to combine. Using a large spoon, stir in the peanut butter until well combined with the dry ingredients.

In a small bowl, combine the milk, egg, vanilla, and melted butter, stirring to break up the egg yolk. Add to the flour mixture, stirring with a large spoon or spatula. Do not beat or overmix. The batter will be thick.

Spoon the batter evenly into the prepared muffin pan. Bake for 25–30 minutes or until a toothpick inserted into a muffin comes out clean. Let the muffins cool completely, then use a spoon to drizzle the melted chocolate on top.

New Year's Day

My mother, a native of Iredell County, North Carolina, had a superstition for every occasion. If I happened to scratch my nose, she'd say company was coming. If the woolly worm bugs had thick coats in the fall, it meant a harsh winter was on the way.

But her biggest bag of beliefs had to do with New Year's Day. She called one of the male neighbors first thing on the first day of each year to ensure that he was our first visitor—it was bad luck if a woman was the first person through the door on the first day of the new year, Mama said.

She insisted on serving the traditional lucky foods of black-eyed peas and collard greens at New Year's. And she insisted that her children eat them so the whole family would get lots of money in the coming year. She was specific: the black-eyed peas were for the "silver money," Mama said, and the greens were for the "folding money."

Not a black-eyed pea fan as a child, I would ask if I could just go for the big bills. No. The luck only works if they're combined, she said. Never argue with an expert.

Apple and Bacon–Stuffed Collard Roll-Ups

My husband, a born and bred southerner, hates collards. I took this attitude as a challenge. This recipe was inspired by Greek stuffed grape leaves, and it received my reluctant collard eater's seal of approval. Use small or cabbage collards for tender leaves.

MAKES 6 APPETIZER SERVINGS

2 cups cooked brown rice

3 tablespoons peeled, finely chopped apples

4 slices cooked bacon, crumbled

3 tablespoons chopped toasted pecans

$\frac{1}{2}$ teaspoon black pepper

$\frac{1}{2}$ teaspoon salt, or to taste

1 tablespoon olive oil

6 small collard leaves

In a bowl, combine the rice, apples, bacon, pecans, pepper, salt, and olive oil.

Steam the collard leaves on a rack over boiling water in a covered pot for about 5 minutes, until they're bright green and soft but not limp. Don't overcook them.

Place a leaf on a cutting board and use a sharp knife to cut away the center stem, cutting each leaf in half lengthwise. Discard the stem. Spoon a scant ¼ cup of the filling in the center of each half. Fold the short ends of the leaf over the filling, then fold the bottom up and roll. Tuck in the top of the leaf and place the roll seam-side down on a serving plate. Repeat with the remaining leaves and filling.

Serve immediately or cover with plastic wrap and refrigerate for up to 2 days.

Sweet Potatoes Restaurant's Quick and Easy Hoppin' John Soup

At one time, downtown Winston-Salem, North Carolina, wasn't a dining destination. That has changed now, and the restaurant Sweet Potatoes is a big part of the revitalization. Chef Stephanie L. Tyson and her partner, Vivian Joiner, offer down-home food with big-city flavor. Stephanie graciously allowed me to include this recipe for a dish that offers a twist on the usual hoppin' John from her book Well, Shut My Mouth! The Sweet Potatoes Restaurant Cookbook, *published by John F. Blair.*

MAKES 8 SERVINGS

½ cup diced celery
1 cup diced yellow onions
½ cup diced green bell peppers
1 tablespoon dried thyme
¼ teaspoon red pepper flakes
½ cup diced country ham
2 tablespoons bacon drippings or vegetable oil
1 teaspoon chopped garlic
2 (15-ounce) cans black-eyed peas
1 quart chicken stock
1 (6-ounce) package frozen collard greens
1½ cups canned diced tomatoes, drained
2 cups cooked rice
Salt and black pepper

In a large saucepan or Dutch oven, sauté the celery, onions, green bell peppers, thyme, pepper flakes, and country ham in the bacon drippings or vegetable oil for about 10 minutes until the vegetables are soft. Add the garlic and cook for 1 minute. Add the black-eyed peas, chicken stock, and collard greens.

Bring to a boil, then reduce the heat to a simmer and cook for 10 minutes. Stir in the tomatoes and rice and heat through. Taste, then add salt and pepper if needed.

Old Christmas

Residents of the North Carolina Outer Banks are an independent bunch. People determined enough to withstand being bashed regularly by storms, to handle the destruction of roads, and to coax a living from an uncooperative sea tend not to put up with nonsense.

In 1752, when the English adopted the Georgian calendar, the isolated settlers didn't hear about it for many years, writes Elizabeth Wiegand in *The Outer Banks Cookbook: Recipes and Traditions from North Carolina's Barrier Islands*. When they did find out, they preferred to continue celebrating Old Christmas, also called Epiphany, as they always had.

Today, Christmas Day is for families and Old Christmas is a community celebration with a reputation for rowdiness that has been toned down. There are shooting contests, costume parades, and an appearance by Old Buck, a bull that according to legend ran wild on the islands, frightening everyone. Islanders make a costume from a cow skull and blankets so that Old Buck can run amok once again and pump up the party.

At one time, swans (called "white turkey") were on the menu. But oysters have always been at the center of Old Christmas celebrations. Sometimes being stubborn is a good thing.

Sassy Cocktail Sauce

Homemade cocktail sauce has a fresher flavor than the bottled stuff, and you can flavor it to suit yourself. I lean toward an abundance of horseradish, but you can follow your own whim.

MAKES ABOUT 1 CUP

1 cup ketchup or chili sauce

¼ teaspoon garlic powder

½ teaspoon Worcestershire sauce

Dash of hot pepper sauce, or to taste

2 heaping tablespoons prepared horseradish

2 teaspoons fresh lemon juice

In a small bowl, stir all ingredients together until well combined. Cover and refrigerate at least 1 hour, until chilled. Stir before serving.

How to Do Your Own Oyster Roast

In The Outer Banks Cookbook: Recipes and Traditions from North Carolina's Barrier Islands, *published by Globe Pequot Press, Elizabeth Wiegand offers these excellent instructions for having an oyster roast at home. It's great but messy fun, so do this outdoors. Look for oyster knives with short, flat blades and sturdy handles; I've found good ones at old-fashioned hardware stores or bait-and-tackle shops.*

SERVES A GOOD-SIZED CROWD

Several pairs of heavy gloves, preferably rubber

1–2 bushels raw oysters

Table or extra-large bucket for rinsing and cleaning oysters

Outside water hose

Scrub brush

Turkey fryer or grill (charcoal or gas)

Outdoor picnic table

Newspapers

Oyster knives

Saltine crackers

Bowls of melted butter and cocktail sauce

Plastic bowls, forks, and cups

Iced tea, bourbon, or beer

Garbage can for shells

Wear thick rubber or work gloves to prevent being cut by the sharp oyster shells. Oyster cuts tend to get infected or, at the least, to be very sore.

Use an old table, a piece of roofing tin on two sawhorses, or an extra-large bucket for the big and wet job of rinsing. Rinse the oysters with cold water and scrub with a brush to remove any mud. All shells should be closed or should close when you handle or tap on them. If any shells remain open, the oyster is dead and should not be eaten.

For steamed oysters, use a turkey fryer. Place the cleaned oysters in the steamer basket, fill the fryer with water to a depth of 3 or 4 inches, and lower the basket into the fryer. Turn on the burner and get the water boiling. Steam for 8–10 minutes or until the oysters open easily. As the oysters begin to open, their juices will feed the steaming water. Check the pot after every batch to make sure you have sufficient water.

For grilled oysters, place the oysters on a hot grill for 8–10 minutes. You may find a grated tray helpful. Remove the oysters from the grill when they open easily.

Cover an outdoor picnic table with newspapers. Have oyster knives ready, along with saltines; bowls of melted butter and cocktail sauce; plastic bowls, forks, and cups; and iced tea, bourbon, or beer. When the oysters are done, dump them directly onto the table.

Enlist the help of several experienced folks to open the oysters, wearing gloves, for your guests. Have them toss the empty shells into a garbage can.

Oyster shells can be used as compost or mulch to fertilize bushes and fruit trees.

Mardi Gras

Many people believe that Mardi Gras is just a big "Girls Gone Wild" video that goes on for weeks. In New Orleans's French Quarter, that might be true. But go outside the areas of tourist-clogged bars—to neighborhoods, suburbs, and smaller towns—and you'll find a colorful celebration that isn't all about chugging Hurricanes.

The Carnival season begins on January 6, Epiphany, and ends on Mardi Gras, the night before Ash Wednesday, when Lent and its period of atonement begin. The concept of Mardi Gras came to heavily Catholic Louisiana in the 1700s, and the first krewe—a social club that organizes balls, parades, and floats—formed in New Orleans then.

In smaller Gulf Coast towns, celebrations are more family-oriented but no less fun. Rural communities in Cajun areas of Louisiana celebrate an old-fashioned variation: masked men knock on doors, singing songs, playing music, and dancing to solicit donations of ingredients for a giant gumbo that is later served to all.

And everywhere you see the traditional Mardi Gras colors: purple, representing justice; gold, representing power; and green, symbolizing faith. The colors always bedeck the traditional dessert of king cake.

Brandy Milk Punch

This recipe is adapted from one I got from the Southern Food and Beverage Museum in New Orleans. Liz Williams of SOFAB says this punch is a favorite for brunches. At 1 ounce of brandy per serving, having one won't knock you out for the rest of the day. My cocktail tester found that using a wire-coil or hawthorne strainer instead of the strainer in the cocktail shaker allowed the pleasant foaminess of this drink to come through.

MAKES 2 DRINKS

2 ounces brandy
1 cup very cold whole milk
1 teaspoon confectioners' sugar
Freshly grated nutmeg

Put the brandy, milk, and confectioners' sugar in a three-piece cobbler cocktail shaker and add three ice cubes. Shake for 1 minute. Remove the strainer portion of the shaker and strain the mixture through a wire-coil or hawthorne strainer into 2 double-old-fashioned glasses. Sprinkle with nutmeg.

Coconut King Cake

Every brunch or party during the long Carnival season features this sweet yeasted coffee cake. Some kinds are rolled with cinnamon, but I prefer filled versions. My filling is not as sweet as some. I add coconut for a different flavor and as a nod to New Orleans's Krewe of Zulu, whose members hand out actual coconuts from their parade floats. Whoever gets the slice of king cake containing a dried bean or charm has to bring the cake to the next party.

MAKES 8–10 SERVINGS

FOR THE DOUGH

1 (¼-ounce) package active dry yeast
2 tablespoons sugar
1 cup milk
2½ cups bread flour
¼ teaspoon salt
½ teaspoon mace or nutmeg
2 large egg yolks, at room temperature
4 tablespoons unsalted butter, at room temperature
Dried bean or charm

FOR THE FILLING

1 (8-ounce) package cream cheese, at room temperature
¾ cup shredded coconut
½ cup confectioners' sugar

FOR THE ICING

¼ cup milk
2 cups confectioners' sugar
¼ teaspoon coconut extract
Colored sugar in purple, yellow or gold, and green,
    for decoration

To make the dough, place the yeast and sugar in the bowl of a stand mixer. Warm the milk until it reaches 110° on an instant-read thermometer, then pour it into the bowl while whisking. Let sit until the mixture foams, about 10 minutes.

In a separate bowl, stir together the flour, salt, and mace or nutmeg.

Gently whisk the egg yolks into the yeast mixture, then whisk in the butter. Add the flour mixture and stir until combined.

Use the dough hook of the stand mixer to work the dough on medium-high speed until it pulls away from the sides of the bowl, 1–2 minutes. Place the dough in a lightly oiled bowl, cover with a lint-free tea towel, and place in a warm, draft-free place to rise until doubled in size, 1½–2 hours.

Meanwhile, prepare the filling. Combine the cream cheese, coconut, and confectioners' sugar and stir until smooth.

When the dough has doubled, turn it out onto a floured work surface. With floured hands, pat it into a rectangle about 6 inches wide and 16–18 inches long. Spread the filling lengthwise just off center of the dough, then fold one long side of the dough over the filling and pinch the edges of the dough together. Place the dough on a baking sheet lined with parchment paper. Bring the ends together to form a ring with the seam side of the rectangle in the center. Pinch the ends of the dough together to seal. Cover with a lint-free tea towel and let rise in a warm, draft-free place until doubled in size, about 1 hour.

Preheat the oven to 350°. When the dough has risen, remove the towel and insert a dried bean or charm into it. Bake the dough for about 30 minutes or until golden brown. Cool on a wire rack.

To make the icing, combine the milk, confectioners' sugar, and coconut extract in a small bowl. When the cake is completely cool, drizzle on the icing, then sprinkle with the colored sugar in alternating colors.

St. Joseph's Day

MARCH 19

When drought and famine threatened the predominantly Catholic people of Sicily during the Middle Ages, they prayed to St. Joseph for help. The rains finally came, and in gratitude, they made the saint's day for Jesus' foster father a time to celebrate abundance and give to those who lack it. They created altars to the saint that were covered with food, which they donated to the poor.

Sicilian immigrants brought the tradition with them to New Orleans in the nineteenth century. As with many things in New Orleans, it was amped up there. Today, area Catholic churches—plus some private homes and at least one bar—construct elaborate altars, some a third the size of a basketball court, filled with Sicilian foods and symbolic items. Because St. Joseph was a carpenter, there are breads in the shapes of saws, ladders, and other carpenters' tools. Cakes decorated to look like lambs, symbolizing Jesus, are common. Plates of seafood often include twelve fish to represent the apostles.

At most altars, each visitor receives a bag with traditional Sicilian cookies and a dried fava bean, which is considered lucky because fava beans fed the population during the famine.

Pasta Milanese with Mudrica

*Many churches offer free buffet meals on St. Joseph's Day, and
most include a version of this traditional Sicilian dish. I adapted
this recipe from one in the* St. Joseph Women's Club Altar Cookbook *from St. Joseph Church in Gretna, Louisiana. The Mudrica
atop the pasta symbolizes sawdust, referring back to St. Joseph's
profession.*

MAKES 8–10 SERVINGS

FOR THE SAUCE
½ cup olive oil
1 large onion, finely chopped
5 garlic cloves, finely chopped
1 (12-ounce) can tomato paste
1 (28-ounce) can crushed tomatoes
⅓ cup chopped fennel
1 teaspoon sugar
2½ tablespoons dried currants
1 (4.25-ounce) can sardines packed in water,
    drained and chopped
Salt and black pepper

FOR THE MUDRICA
Olive oil
3 cups fine dried bread crumbs
1 tablespoon sugar

Cooked spaghetti

To make the sauce, heat the olive oil in a large saucepan. Sauté the onion and garlic until soft. Add the tomato paste, crushed tomatoes, and fennel. Add 3 cups water, the sugar, and the currants. Simmer, uncovered, over medium heat until the sauce begins to thicken, about 5 minutes.

Add the sardines. Cover and cook over medium-low heat until the sauce is thick, about 1 hour. Taste and add salt and pepper as needed.

To make the Mudrica, put enough olive oil in a large skillet to just cover the bottom and warm on medium heat. Add the bread crumbs and sugar. Cook, stirring constantly, a few minutes until the mixture is light brown.

Serve the sauce over cooked spaghetti and top with Mudrica.

Cuccidati

These cookies with a fig filling are traditional on every St. Joseph's Day altar, and they're usually in the gift bags given to visitors. The filling can be made a day ahead and refrigerated, if necessary. Don't put too much filling in the cookies — a small strip down the center of the dough is enough. I adapted this recipe from one in the St. Joseph Women's Club Altar Cookbook from St. Joseph Church in Gretna, Louisiana. Look for dried figs and good-quality candied orange peel at Middle Eastern markets.

MAKES 40–50 COOKIES

FOR THE FILLING

2 cups dried figs, stems removed
1 cup chopped pecans ¾ cup raisins
1¼ cups candied orange peel
¼ teaspoon cinnamon
¼ teaspoon nutmeg
¼ teaspoon black pepper
½ orange, peeled and chopped into chunks,
    seeds removed
½ lemon, peeled and chopped into chunks,
    seeds removed
Orange juice (if needed)

FOR THE DOUGH

1½ cups sugar
1 cup vegetable shortening or margarine
5 large eggs
½ cup evaporated milk
¾ teaspoon vanilla
8 cups flour
4 tablespoons baking powder

Preheat the oven to 375°.

To make the filling, toss together the figs, pecans, raisins, candied orange peel, cinnamon, nutmeg, and black pepper. Put the mixture through a meat grinder, adding enough lemon and orange chunks to make a stiff but moist filling. Add a little orange juice if the filling seems too dry and won't hold together. The filling can be covered and refrigerated overnight at this point.

To make the dough, place the sugar and shortening or margarine in the bowl of a stand mixer and beat until fluffy and combined. In a separate bowl, combine the eggs, evaporated milk, and vanilla. Add the egg mixture to the sugar and shortening mixture and beat to combine. On low speed, gradually add the flour and baking powder and stir until combined. You will have a stiff dough.

On a lightly floured surface, roll about a third of the dough into a ⅛-inch-thick strip about 3 inches wide. It's easier to work in batches rather than rolling out all the dough at once. Spread a small strip of filling down the center of the dough. Fold one long side over and press the edges to seal firmly. If the dough tears, simply press it back together. Cut crosswise into 2-inch pieces. Press the dough together over the cut edges and place, seam-side down, on a nonstick cookie sheet. Cut two small slits in each cookie to let the steam escape. Bake for 15–20 minutes or until the cookies are light brown.

March Madness

Come on—y'all know it's a holiday.

The squeak of the sneaker and thump of the roundball are heard from one end of the South to the other as sports fans center their lives around tip-off times, if their teams are lucky enough to play in the NCAA men's college basketball tournament.

March has been madness in North Carolina for decades. With fierce rivals Duke University, North Carolina State University, and the University of North Carolina mere miles apart, the ACC Tournament in early March is an epic event. The SEC Tournament throws together the University of Kentucky and the University of Tennessee. Travel around the region and you will find a steaming stew of fan fervor.

Office workers take long lunches at sports bars or gather around televisions or computer screens. The boss doesn't care— she's watching, too. At home, the traditional midday Sunday start of the ACC final is a perfect occasion to cook up a brunch fit for winners. Evening games require the right snacks. No matter which team wins, you can be certain that southern basketball fans will feed their friends right. The quality of the food affects the outcome of the game, right?

Very Veggie Brunch Casserole

Vegetarians are sports fans, too. This do-ahead casserole for brunch or dinner has so much flavor that it makes carnivores happy, too. Feel free to use frozen asparagus if fresh isn't available.

MAKES 10 SERVINGS

8 slices challah or potato bread, crust removed and
   cut into cubes
4 tablespoons unsalted butter, melted
2 cups shredded Mexican-blend cheese
3 cups chopped cooked asparagus
1 large red bell pepper, chopped
3 green onions, chopped
2 cups milk (whole or 2%, not fat-free)
4 large eggs
1 teaspoon salt
1½ teaspoons black pepper

Toss the bread cubes with the melted butter. Spread half of the bread cubes in the bottom of a buttered 9 × 13-inch baking dish. On top of the bread, spread half of the cheese, then all of the asparagus, red bell pepper, and green onions. Top with the remaining cheese and bread cubes.

In a large bowl, whisk together the milk, eggs, salt, and pepper. Pour the mixture over the casserole, cover with foil, and refrigerate overnight.

When ready to cook, preheat the oven to 350°. To speed baking, let the casserole come to room temperature. Bake for 30 minutes, then remove the foil and bake for another 45 minutes to 1 hour or until the top is brown.

Smokin' Mary

A great bloody mary is required for any game-day brunch. I created this smoky version by adding chipotle peppers. For the best flavor, shun salty mixers and canned juices and look for a bottled, no-salt-added pure tomato juice. It's also quite easy to make your own tomato juice. Cut about 4 pounds of fresh tomatoes into quarters and purée them in a blender, then strain to remove the skins and seeds. This should give you 1 quart of juice. A version of this recipe originally appeared in my cookbook Fan Fare: A Playbook of Great Recipes for Tailgating or Watching the Game at Home, *published by Harvard Common Press. Serve them in University of North Carolina cups, of course.*

MAKES 6–8 DRINKS

1 quart tomato juice
1½ tablespoons chipotle purée (see Note)
⅓ cup fresh lime juice
1½ teaspoons salt, or to taste
1 teaspoon garlic powder
Vodka
Cilantro sprigs and lime slices

Combine the tomato juice, chipotle purée, lime juice, salt, and garlic powder in a large pitcher. Stir well to combine. To serve, pour the mixture into tall glasses filled with ice and stir in the desired amount of vodka. Add a cilantro sprig to each glass and garnish the rim with a lime slice.

NOTE ❋ To make chipotle purée, put a can of chipotle peppers in adobo sauce in a blender and process until smooth.

Spring

THERE'S HAM ON THE EASTER TABLE, AND SEAFOOD ABOUNDS AS FLEETS SET SAIL FOR THE SEASON

Holidays and festivals celebrate rebirth and renewal with fresh things arriving at farmers' markets.

Blessing of the Fleet

EARLY SPRING

When spring fishing season opens, communities across the coastal South hold Blessing of the Fleet celebrations. They're like block parties but with boats. Fishing vessels are decorated with colorful flags, music and food abound, and local clergy offer prayers for an abundant and safe season.

In Bayou La Batre, Alabama, St. Margaret's Church has been holding the celebration since 1949. Each year, the ladies of the church hand-stitch a fleet blessing quilt with a nautical theme that's raffled off to raise money for church projects. And, of course, there's plenty of good food.

The faces of southern fishermen may have changed over the decades—many are Vietnamese immigrants now—but St. Margaret's traditional fleet blessing prayer is the same: "May God in heaven fulfill abundantly the prayers which are pronounced over you and your boats and equipment on the occasion of the Blessing of the Fleet. God bless your going out and coming in, and the Lord be with you at home and on the water. May he accompany you when you start on your many journeys. May he fill your nets abundantly as a reward for your labor. And may he bring you all safely in when you turn your boats homeward to shore."

Vietnamese Spring Rolls

This is my homage to the Vietnamese families who work much of the Gulf Coast fishing grounds today. These rolls are easy to make and refreshing on a steamy day.

MAKES 5 ROLLS

1 ounce bean thread noodles

5 rice paper wrappers

½ cup finely shredded carrots

½ large cucumber, peeled, seeded, and thinly sliced

5 green onion tops

10 medium shrimp, cooked, shelled, deveined,
   and cut in half lengthwise

15–20 mint leaves

20–25 cilantro leaves

¼ cup creamy peanut butter

1 tablespoon fresh lemon or lime juice

1 tablespoon fish sauce

2 tablespoons rice vinegar

Hot sauce

Put 2–3 cups of water in a saucepan and bring to a boil. Remove the boiling water from the heat and add the bean thread noodles. There should be enough water to cover the noodles. Let sit for 10 minutes or until the noodles are soft. Drain in a colander, rinse under cold water, and let drain thoroughly. Make sure the noodles are at room temperature before using.

To assemble the rolls, place a large bowl of hot tap water beside a cutting board. Arrange all your ingredients within reach. Dip a rice paper wrapper in the hot water for a few seconds, until it softens, then place it on the cutting board. Add a fifth of the carrots and cucumber, 1 green onion top, 4 shrimp halves, 3 or 4 mint leaves, 4 or 5 cilantro leaves, and a fifth of the noodles. Fold the bottom and the top of the wrapper over the filling, then roll up the sides. Place on a serving plate, seam-side down. Repeat with the remaining ingredients.

To make the dipping sauce, combine the peanut butter, lemon or lime juice, fish sauce, and rice vinegar in a small bowl. Add hot sauce to taste.

Serve the spring rolls immediately with the dipping sauce or cover the plate tightly with plastic wrap to prevent the rolls from drying out and refrigerate for up to 4 hours.

Seafood Gumbo

This gumbo is packed with good things from the sea and makes enough to feed a fleet of hungry people. Feel free to cut the recipe in half if your crew is smaller. I adapted this recipe from one in Sharing Our Catch, *a cookbook from the Ladies Society of St. Margaret's Church in Bayou La Batre, Alabama.*

MAKES 12 SERVINGS

1 cup vegetable oil or bacon drippings

1 cup flour

2 medium onions, chopped

2 stalks celery, chopped

1 large green bell pepper, chopped

6 garlic cloves, minced

1 gallon chicken broth

4 cups sliced okra

Salt and black pepper

1 pint oysters, undrained

1 pound claw crabmeat

2 pounds medium shrimp, peeled and deveined

$\frac{1}{2}$ cup chopped parsley

$\frac{1}{2}$ cup chopped green onion tops

Cooked rice

Filé

Make a roux by combining the vegetable oil or bacon drippings and flour in a large, heavy pot over medium heat. Cook, stirring constantly, until the roux is the color of a copper penny, 10–15 minutes. Do not stop stirring at any time. Adjust the heat if the roux is cooking too fast. Do not burn the roux, because it will ruin the gumbo. If you see any burned black specks, discard the roux, wash the pot, and start over.

When the roux is the proper color, add the onions, celery, green bell pepper, and garlic. Cook, stirring constantly, until the vegetables are tender. Reduce the heat if necessary.

Warm the chicken broth in a saucepan, then gradually add the warm chicken broth to the roux mixture in small amounts, blending well after each addition. Add the okra. Bring the mixture to a boil, then reduce the heat and simmer, uncovered, for 1 hour. Taste and add salt and pepper as needed. Add all the seafood, then bring to a boil, reduce the heat, and simmer for 10–15 minutes or until the seafood is cooked through. Top with the parsley and green onion tops, then serve over rice. Pass filé at the table.

Passover

MID-MARCH OR EARLY APRIL

After my husband and I got engaged, he took me to my first Passover seder. He had told me that there was a meal involved and that it took a long time to get around to eating because everyone had to read aloud the story of the Jews' flight from Egypt. He neglected to mention that I would need a dictionary for the menu.

I spent much of the evening whispering in his ear. Because we were newly engaged, his family assumed we were billing and cooing. Actually, I was asking, "What's that?" about practically every other dish. Now I know them all and put my own twist on the traditions.

Similar to Easter, Passover's date is based on lunar cycles and therefore moves around. One year, it fell on the night of the NCAA men's college basketball championship game, in which our beloved University of North Carolina at Chapel Hill Tar Heels were playing. My mother-in-law hosted the gathering at her home in Chapel Hill, and because she was a fan as well, the seder zipped along like an open-court fast break. We finished by tip-off and were conveniently located in front of the television in time to celebrate the Heels' victory. That's what I call a holiday.

Matzoh Balls, Cajun Style

For generations, southern Jewish cooks have added new accents to old traditions. If you love lots of flavor, as they do in Louisiana, why would you leave it out for Passover? This recipe was inspired by one I got from Carol Anne Blitzer in Baton Rouge. She says, "We consider matzoh balls in other parts of the country to be very bland." These will liven up the old chicken soup.

MAKES ABOUT 20 MATZOH BALLS

1/2 medium onion

2 green onions, white and green parts

10–12 stems parsley

3 tablespoons olive oil or vegetable oil

1 1/4 cups matzoh meal

1/2 teaspoon salt

1/2 teaspoon cayenne pepper

3/4 cup chicken broth

2 large eggs, lightly beaten

Place the onion, green onions, and parsley in a food processor and pulse until finely chopped.

Heat the olive oil or vegetable oil in a sauté pan over medium heat. Add the vegetables and cook, stirring, until fragrant and lightly brown. Place the vegetables in a large bowl.

In another bowl, mix together the matzoh meal, salt, and cayenne pepper. Add to the vegetables along with the chicken broth and eggs. Stir until combined. Cover the bowl with plastic wrap and refrigerate for at least 2 hours.

Use your hands to roll the thoroughly chilled dough into walnut-sized balls. You may cook them at this point or freeze them for later use by putting the balls on a cookie sheet and placing them in the freezer. When the balls are frozen hard, transfer them to a reclosable plastic bag and store them in the freezer until needed. Cook the frozen matzoh balls directly from the freezer; do not thaw.

To cook, bring a large pot of water to a rolling boil, then add the matzoh balls. Return the water to a boil, reduce the heat to a medium simmer, and cover the pot. Cook for 30–40 minutes or until the matzoh balls are cooked through.

Sephardic Matzoh Lasagna

My husband bemoans most matzoh-based dishes that show up during the eight days of Passover, when leavened bread is banned. But he likes this lasagna, with its exotic flavor and texture, so much that it may show up year-round. I adapted this recipe from one in a Passover recipe pamphlet from Temple Mickve Israel in Savannah, Georgia.

MAKES 8 SERVINGS

1 pound ground beef

1 pound ground turkey

2 tablespoons cinnamon, divided

½ cup olive oil, divided

1 medium onion, chopped

1 pound mushrooms, sliced

Salt and black pepper

1 large eggplant, peeled and cut into 1-inch cubes

3 garlic cloves, chopped

2 (15-ounce) cans tomato sauce, divided

1 tablespoon sugar

6 large eggs, lightly beaten

6–7 matzohs

Preheat the oven to 350°. Spray a 9 × 13-inch baking dish with nonstick cooking spray.

In a large frying pan over medium heat, cook the ground beef and turkey until browned. Add a little olive oil if they stick at first. Drain well and place in a large bowl. Sprinkle on 1 tablespoon of the cinnamon and stir.

Add ¼ cup of the olive oil to the pan and return to medium heat. Cook the onion, stirring, until soft. Add the mushrooms and a little salt and pepper and cook, stirring, until the mushrooms are soft. Place the vegetables in a medium bowl.

Add the remaining ¼ cup olive oil to the pan and cook the eggplant and garlic, stirring, until the eggplant is soft. Add the eggplant mixture to the onion and mushroom mixture. Stir the remaining 1 tablespoon cinnamon into the mixture. Stir the eggplant mixture into the meat, then stir in 1 can of the tomato sauce and the sugar. Taste the filling, then add salt and pepper if needed.

Spread a thin layer of tomato sauce on the bottom of the prepared baking dish. Prepare to assemble the lasagna by lining up a shallow dish of hot tap water, several layers of paper towels, a shallow dish with the beaten eggs, and the baking dish. Dip a matzoh in the hot water just long enough for it to soften. It's OK to break it in half. Lay the soaked matzoh on the paper towels to drain briefly, then dip it in the egg and lay it on the bottom of the baking dish. Repeat with another matzoh. Two standard matzohs should cover the bottom of the baking dish. Spread half of the filling evenly over the matzohs. Top the filling with a third of the remaining can of tomato sauce. Repeat with another layer of matzohs, filling, and tomato sauce. Top the second layer with matzohs, then the remaining tomato sauce.

Bake for 40 minutes or until the top is firm.

Easter

MARCH OR APRIL

One spring day, my husband asked me why southerners always have ham at Easter. (It's certainly not a biblical mandate.) I didn't know, so I did some research.

The Easter ham appears to be a tradition born of timing. In the days before refrigeration, farmers would kill hogs when the weather got cold in late fall, then salt the hams and hang them up to cure for several months. Curing the hams preserved the meat, according to *The Country Ham Book* by Jeanne Voltz and Elaine J. Harvell, published by the University of North Carolina Press. During the ensuing winter, the only meat families might have was game. The hams generally would be ready to eat around Easter, and ham would be a much-anticipated part of a holiday meal.

Today, people line up to buy spiral-sliced, sticky-sweet "city hams" for Easter. (I will not even entertain the thought of canned hams; I hope my mother was the last person on Earth to serve those.) Although convenient, spiral-sliced hams lack the rich complexity of good-quality country hams, which require some preparation before serving but bring a unique flavor and texture to dishes. And country hams are more a part of the history of Easter in the South than that egg-toting rabbit.

Hop-into-Spring Deviled Eggs

As Easter approached, my father would sing as an early form of rap, "Eastertime is the time for eggs, and the time for eggs is Eastertime." Easter without deviled eggs is—well, it's just not done. My first cookbook was all about deviled eggs, but here's a new recipe, because deviled eggs are infinite.

MAKES 12 DEVILED EGGS

6 large eggs

½ cup soft herb-garlic-flavored cheese, such as Boursin, at room temperature

2 tablespoons sour cream

¼ cup chopped toasted pecans, plus more for garnish

½ teaspoon black pepper

Salt

Place the eggs in one layer in a saucepan and cover them completely with cold water. Place the saucepan over high heat and bring to a boil. When the water reaches a boil, remove the saucepan from the heat and cover with a lid. Let sit for 15 minutes, then drain the eggs and cool them quickly under cold running water or by putting them in a bowl of ice water.

When the eggs have cooled, peel them, cut them in half lengthwise, and place the yolks in a bowl. Mash the yolks with a fork. Stir in the cheese, the sour cream, ¼ cup pecans, and the pepper. Taste and add salt as needed.

Spoon the filling evenly into the egg white halves. Garnish each egg half with a few pieces of toasted pecans.

Jeanne's Slow-Cooker Country Ham

One of my first advisers as a brand-new food editor was Jeanne Voltz. After working for the Miami Herald, Woman's Day, *and the* Los Angeles Times *and writing several cookbooks, she retired near Raleigh and was always willing to answer even the silliest question. I adapted this recipe from her* The Country Ham Book, *which she coauthored with Elaine J. Harvell, published by the University of North Carolina Press. Be sure to ask for the shank end of the ham, not the end with the hock. A good butcher will be willing to sell you half a country ham, which is enough for a small family. If you're feeding a mob, do what the original recipe suggests: cook both halves using two slow-cookers.*

MAKES ABOUT 10 SERVINGS

Half of the shank end of a country ham (about 7 pounds)
1½ cups cola

If you see any mold on the ham, scrub it off with a stiff brush. (You often see mold on a ham; no need to throw it away.) In a large bowl or a clean kitchen sink, completely immerse the ham in cold water and let it soak for 1 hour.

Spray the crockery insert of a large slow-cooker with nonstick cooking spray. Remove the ham from the water and place it in the cooker. Pour the cola over the ham and cover it with the lid. If the ham keeps the lid from fitting, trim a bit of fat off the ham with a sharp knife until the lid fits or cover the edges of the lid with foil to seal it. As the ham cooks, it will shrink and the lid will fit on its own. Cook on low for 2 hours.

After 2 hours, turn the ham, ladle the liquid in the cooker over it, replace the cover, and cook on low for 2 more hours.

Remove the ham from the slow-cooker and let it cool to room temperature before slicing. You can also wrap the ham tightly and refrigerate it, but bring it to room temperature before serving.

Slice the ham thin and serve on biscuits or crackers or use in casseroles, omelets, etc.

Hot Cross Buns

These are an Easter tradition in areas with a Moravian presence. As a kid, I adored the buns from a local bakery because they were basically sugar-delivery vehicles. Candied fruit studded the sweet bread, which was topped with a cross made with thick icing. My version is less sweet with more spice but still great for Easter breakfast.

MAKES 16 BUNS

½ cup milk

½ cup granulated sugar

1 teaspoon salt

2 (¼-ounce) packages active dry yeast

3¼ cups bread flour, divided

2 large eggs plus 1 large egg white, divided

1 stick unsalted butter, melted and cooled to
   room temperature

½ teaspoon cinnamon

½ teaspoon cardamom

1 tablespoon grated lemon zest

¾ cup raisins

1 cup confectioners' sugar

Dash of vanilla

Warm the milk in a saucepan over medium-low heat until it steams and bubbles form where it touches the pan, but do not let it boil. Pour it into the bowl of a stand mixer. Add the granulated sugar and salt and stir until the sugar dissolves. Let cool to lukewarm.

Meanwhile, place ¼ cup warm water (105°–115°) in a small bowl and stir in the yeast. Let sit for 5 minutes or until it foams, then add to the milk mixture. Add 1¼ cups of the flour and, using the dough hook, beat on medium-low speed for 2–3 minutes, until the dough comes together. Beat in 2 eggs and the melted butter. Then add the remaining 2 cups flour plus the cinnamon, cardamom, and lemon zest. Beat for 2–3 minutes, until the dough is smooth; don't overbeat.

Cover the bowl with a lint-free tea towel and put in a warm, draft-free place to rise until doubled in size, about 1½ hours. Work in the raisins, adding a little more flour if needed to make a soft dough. Return the dough to the bowl, cover it with plastic wrap, and refrigerate for at least 3 hours or overnight.

Place the dough on a lightly floured surface and knead for a few minutes. Then, using a knife or dough scraper, divide it into 4 pieces. Roll one piece into a thick log shape and cut it into 4 pieces, then roll each piece into a bun. Place the buns on a greased 9 × 13-inch pan or other baking pan with sides. Position them very close together or even touching. Repeat with the remaining dough. Mix the egg white with a teaspoon or so of cold water, then brush the tops of the buns with the egg white mixture. Cover with a lint-free tea towel and let rise until doubled in size, about 2 hours.

Preheat the oven to 350°. Bake the buns for 15–20 minutes or until browned. Let the buns cool to room temperature before frosting.

Make the frosting by combining the confectioners' sugar with a couple of teaspoons of water, just enough to make a thick frosting. Stir in the vanilla. Using the tip of a spoon or a pastry bag, draw crosses on top of the buns with the frosting.

Market Fresh Potato Salad

Serving ham with potato salad creates a heavenly combination, a perfect balance of salty-savory and creamy-rich. This recipe uses the spring bounty. New potatoes are the first freshly dug potatoes of spring and are about the size of golf balls.

MAKES 6 SERVINGS

2 pounds unpeeled new potatoes

1 cup cooked small green peas

$\frac{1}{2}$ cup chopped green onions, white and green parts

2 large hard-cooked eggs, chopped

$\frac{1}{2}$ cup sour cream

1 tablespoon mayonnaise

$1\frac{1}{2}$ teaspoons fresh lemon juice

$\frac{1}{2}$ teaspoon salt

$\frac{1}{2}$ teaspoon black pepper

2 tablespoons pickled capers, rinsed and drained

2 tablespoons chopped Italian parsley

Wash the potatoes, place them whole in a large pot of water, and bring the water to a boil. Boil the potatoes until they are pierced easily with a fork, 15–20 minutes. Drain and let them cool until you can handle them, then cut them into quarters or halves, depending on the size of the potatoes.

In a large bowl, combine the potatoes, peas, green onions, and eggs. In a small bowl, stir together the sour cream, mayonnaise, lemon juice, salt, and pepper. Pour the dressing over the vegetables and stir to combine. Gently stir in the capers, then top with the parsley.

Summer

SOUTHERNERS CELEBRATE SPECIAL FOODS
AND MOMENTS IN HISTORY

The region's bounty bursts forth like

Fourth of July fireworks, and southerners celebrate

freedom in many forms.

Peach Festivals

THROUGHOUT THE SUMMER

The South's passion for peaches can get a little crazy sometimes.

Gaffney, South Carolina, needed a new water tower and wanted to promote the state's favorite fruit. So in 1981, the town built the Peachoid. I think it looks more like a sassy body part than a fruit, but see for yourself. It's off Interstate 85 near the exit for South Carolina Highway 11.

In Atlanta, a giant peach drops from the top of a downtown building on New Year's Eve. At the Georgia Peach Festival in Peach County, visitors can sample the world's largest peach cobbler: 11 feet long, 5 feet wide, and about 8 inches deep, with 75 gallons of peaches.

Peaches have been grown in the South since the sixteenth century. Georgia and South Carolina have a little feud going on about which state grows the best-tasting peaches. I believe the best peach is the ripest one that traveled the shortest distance to get to me. Clingstones—whose pits don't pop easily from the flesh—ripen first. The freestones arrive in the hottest part of the summer and are so juicy that I just stand over the sink and bite into them.

I guess I'm a little crazy, too.

Peach and Prosciutto Salad

Peaches. Pork. Two of my favorite things. And this salad has that great sweet-salty thing going on. I like the color and sweetness of white peaches for the dish, but use the best, super ripe local peaches of any color that you can find. This is a favorite lunch salad for me for as long as the fresh peaches hold out.

MAKES 5–6 SIDE DISH SERVINGS
OR 2–3 MAIN DISH SERVINGS

- 1 tablespoon fresh lemon juice
- 3 tablespoons olive oil
- 1/4 teaspoon salt
- 1/4 teaspoon black pepper
- 3 cups baby salad greens
- 4 medium ripe peaches (white if possible),
  peeled and cut into quarters
- 1 ball fresh mozzarella
- 4 slices prosciutto
- 2 tablespoons chopped toasted pecans
- 1 teaspoon chopped mint leaves

In a small bowl, whisk together the lemon juice, olive oil, salt, and pepper until combined. In a large bowl, toss the baby salad greens with a tablespoon or so of the dressing, just enough to moisten the greens. Spread the greens on a large plate or platter.

Arrange the peach quarters attractively on top of the greens. Chop the mozzarella into approximately 1-inch chunks, then scatter them around the peaches. Cut or tear the prosciutto into wide shreds and place them on top of the peaches and mozzarella. Sprinkle on another tablespoon or so of the dressing, but don't drown the salad in it. Top with the pecans and mint. Serve the remaining dressing on the side in case diners want more.

Creamy Peach Parfaits

A smooth custard is great on a hot day. My husband recently found out that he's allergic to dairy products, so I came up with this milk-free version that has a mild coconut flavor to accent the peaches. Use milk if you prefer. So easy, so peachy, so cool—and no need to heat up the oven when it's already 95° outside.

MAKES 6–8 SERVINGS

2 cups peeled, chopped ripe peaches

$\frac{1}{2}$ teaspoon cinnamon

$\frac{1}{4}$ teaspoon cardamom

2 tablespoons cornstarch

$\frac{2}{3}$ cup sugar

Pinch of salt

2 cups canned unsweetened coconut milk

3 large egg yolks

$\frac{1}{2}$ teaspoon vanilla

6–8 teaspoons toasted coconut, divided

6–8 teaspoons chopped toasted pecans, divided

Place the peaches, cinnamon, and cardamom in a bowl and toss to combine.

In a heavy saucepan, whisk together the cornstarch, sugar, and salt, breaking up any lumps. Whisk in the coconut milk until the dry ingredients, especially the cornstarch, are dissolved. Thoroughly whisk in the egg yolks. Place the saucepan over medium heat and cook, whisking occasionally, until the mixture reaches a simmer. Continue to cook, whisking constantly, for another 4–5 minutes or until the custard thickens and smoothly coats the back of a spoon. Remove the saucepan from the heat and whisk in the vanilla.

Divide the peaches among 6–8 heat-resistant mugs or cups. Using a ladle, pour the custard evenly over the peaches. If necessary, poke around the peaches with a skewer to make sure the custard gets all the way in among the fruit. Cover the cups with plastic wrap and refrigerate 4–5 hours or until thoroughly chilled. Sprinkle a teaspoon of toasted coconut and a teaspoon of pecans on top of the custard in each cup just before serving.

Ginger-Peach Soda

Peach, ginger, and cardamom are three of my favorite flavors, and they're all here in this cool beverage. Make sure to use fully ripe peaches that will provide lots of tasty juice.

MAKES ABOUT 4 DRINKS

1 cup peeled, thinly sliced ginger
1½ teaspoons cardamom seeds
1 cup sugar
3 large ripe peaches (see Note)
Chilled club soda
Mint sprigs or lime wedges (optional)

Bring the ginger, cardamom seeds, and 1¼ cups water to a boil in a saucepan. When the mixture boils, cover the saucepan and reduce the heat to a low simmer. Let the liquid simmer for about 30 minutes.

Strain the liquid into a saucepan through a strainer lined with cheesecloth. Discard the solids. You should have about 1 cup of liquid. Bring the liquid and the sugar to a boil, stirring constantly to dissolve the sugar. When the sugar is dissolved, remove the pan from the heat and let it cool to room temperature. When the liquid is cool, put it in a covered container or squeeze bottle and refrigerate until cold.

Peel the peaches and remove the pits. Purée the flesh in a blender, then strain the juice through a fine-mesh strainer or food mill. You should end up with about 1 cup of juice. Discard the solids and store the juice, covered, in the refrigerator.

To make each drink, stir together 3–4 tablespoons peach juice, depending on how much peach flavor you want, and ¼ cup chilled ginger-cardamom syrup. Fill a tall glass with ice and pour the mixture over the ice, followed by 1 cup club soda. Stir gently with an iced-tea spoon to combine. Garnish with a mint sprig or lime wedge, if desired.

NOTE ❊ Bottled peach nectar can be substituted for the peach juice, but the flavor will not be as fresh. Add vodka (plain or vanilla) for a sassy cocktail. The syrup will keep in the refrigerator for up to 1 week.

Juneteenth

JUNE 19

It used to take a while for news to travel, even such important news as the Emancipation Proclamation. On June 19, 1865, more than two years after the proclamation was enacted and more than two months after the Civil War ended, a Union army commander told a Galveston, Texas, crowd that all slaves were freed. This made Galveston the site of one of the first readings of the proclamation in the South.

The event, given the name Juneteenth, has been celebrated in Galveston ever since. The holiday has spread to communities across the country, but the city still hosts one of the largest celebrations, which includes the reading of the proclamation, prayer services, parades, concerts, and other activities. In 1979, the Texas legislature established Juneteenth as a state holiday.

Family and community picnics are commonplace on Juneteenth, which means that there's lots of good old southern dishes around. You'll see a lot of red foods, too. According to African American food historian Adrian Miller, the reason for the red foods is unknown, but it may have something to do with the fact that a number of traditional African drinks are red and with the importance of the color red in African society.

Smoky Red Rice

This richly colored dish is good warm or at room temperature, which makes it good for taking to a family dinner or picnic. Using smoked paprika offers the smoky flavor of bacon or ham without the meat.

MAKES 6 SERVINGS

2 tablespoons olive oil
¼ cup chopped green bell peppers
½ cup chopped onions
1 teaspoon chopped garlic
1 (14½-ounce) can diced tomatoes
2 cups chicken broth
1 teaspoon dried thyme, crushed
1 cup uncooked white rice
½ teaspoon salt
1 teaspoon smoked paprika
¼ teaspoon cayenne pepper
2 tablespoons chopped Italian parsley

Place the olive oil in a large saucepan over medium heat. Add the green bell peppers, onions, and garlic and cook, stirring, until the vegetables are soft but not brown.

Add the tomatoes with their liquid, chicken broth, and thyme and bring to a boil. When the mixture is boiling, add the rice and salt. Cover the pan and reduce the heat to a simmer. Simmer for about 15 minutes or until the rice is cooked. Stir in the smoked paprika and cayenne pepper, then garnish with the chopped parsley.

Nanticoke Catfish

Adrian Miller's book Soul Food: The Surprising Story of an American Cuisine, One Plate at a Time, *published by the University of North Carolina Press, is a detailed and fascinating exploration of the history and culture of African American food. Miller writes that there is a long tradition of holding fish fries for community celebrations such as church events, Juneteenth, and the Fourth of July. Miller says this recipe originally appeared in a publication called* The Chesapeake Bay through Ebony Eyes *and that Nanticoke was the name of a Native American tribe in the area.*

MAKES 8 SERVINGS

1½ cups all-purpose flour
¼ cup cornmeal
1 tablespoon rubbed sage
1 tablespoon cayenne pepper, or to taste
1 teaspoon garlic powder
1 teaspoon onion powder
½ teaspoon nutmeg
1 teaspoon salt
1 teaspoon black pepper
4 large eggs
8 catfish fillets
Vegetable oil
Lemon wedges

Mix the flour, cornmeal, sage, cayenne pepper, garlic powder, onion powder, nutmeg, salt, and pepper in a shallow bowl or pie plate. In another shallow bowl or pie plate, whisk the eggs until well beaten.

Rinse the catfish fillets under cold running water and pat them dry.

Preheat the oven to 250°. Set a wire rack inside a rimmed baking sheet lined with paper towels.

Pour vegetable oil to a depth of ½ inch in a large, deep skillet. Heat the oil over medium-high heat until shimmering hot but not smoking.

Dip the fillets into the eggs and let the excess drip off. Dredge them in the flour mixture and gently shake off the excess.

Working in batches to avoid overfilling the skillet, slip the fillets into the hot oil. Fry the fillets, turning once, about 4 minutes on each side, until the coating is crisp and golden brown and the fish is opaque in the center. Transfer the cooked fillets to the wire rack and keep them warm in the oven until all of the fish is fried.

Serve hot with lemon wedges.

Rosy Roselle Sipper

For an alcohol-free version of this drink, replace the rum and curaçao with orange juice. If you prefer a sweeter drink, add more roselle syrup. Also, try adding a shot of the syrup to lemonade or iced tea. Look for dried roselle, which is also called hibiscus or flor de jamaica, in Latin American markets or supermarket ethnic food aisles.

MAKES 2 DRINKS

FOR THE ROSELLE SYRUP
½ cup sugar
2 tablespoons dried roselle

FOR THE DRINKS
3 ounces white rum
1 ounce curaçao
½ ounce fresh lemon juice
Chilled seltzer water or club soda

To make the roselle syrup, place the sugar, the roselle, and ½ cup water in a small saucepan and bring to a rolling boil. Remove from the heat and steep for 30 minutes. Strain, discard the solids, and cool the syrup to room temperature before using. Refrigerate the syrup if not using immediately.

To make the drinks, combine the rum, the curaçao, 2 ounces roselle syrup, and the lemon juice in a cocktail shaker with lots of ice. Shake well, then strain into two old-fashioned glasses filled with ice. Add a dash of seltzer water or club soda to each glass and stir gently.

Independence Day

JULY 4

This holiday arrives when the bounty of summer vegetables is exploding in backyard gardens and at farmers' markets. The best of the season's tomatoes are ready, as are fat ears of sweet corn and cool melons. The annual flood of zucchini hasn't begun, which means no one is trying to get rid of it; they're just enjoying it.

It's hot around here. But with this abundance of goodness to enjoy, southerners can deal with a little toasty heat. Parks and lakes are packed on Independence Day as people use the holiday as a time for family reunions and neighborhood block parties.

Right after the Civil War, Independence Day was not embraced by some southerners who felt it was a northern holiday. Also, July 4, 1863, was when the forty-day siege of Vicksburg, Mississippi, ended with surrender to the Union army. Vicksburg didn't officially celebrate the holiday for about eighty years.

Today, southerners celebrate the Fourth much as those in other parts of the country do, with fireworks, parades, and good food, perhaps savoring the day a bit more due to the sizable number of servicemen and -women based in the region.

Chef & the Farmer's Sugar Baby Watermelon Salad with Jalapeño Vinaigrette

Chef Vivian Howard does fantastic things with fresh, local produce (and other things) at the Kinston, North Carolina, restaurant she runs with her husband, Ben Knight. The awards the restaurant has received confirm that I'm not alone in my opinion (see chefandthefarmer.com for more). Howard prepared this salad at a Southern Foodways Alliance event, and I begged her for the recipe. I use only 1 tablespoon each of sugar and honey in my dressing because I prefer a tart flavor, but adjust for the sweetness you prefer and the heat of your jalapeños. Use the ripest, sweetest local watermelon you can find—Sugar Baby is a popular eastern North Carolina melon. Pack the ingredients for this salad in a cooler, and it makes a sophisticated picnic dish.

MAKES 4 SERVINGS

---

1 large or 2 small jalapeños

⅓ cup extra-virgin olive oil

½ teaspoon salt

¼ cup apple cider vinegar

1–2 tablespoons sugar

1–2 tablespoons honey

16 (1-inch-square) cubes watermelon, large seeds removed and chilled very cold

Fleur de sel or other coarse sea salt

4 heaping tablespoons crumbled feta cheese

Place the jalapeños on a baking sheet and put under the broiler. Roast the jalapeños, turning with tongs, until they are blistered on all sides. This will take only a few minutes. Place the jalapeños in a plastic bag and seal. Let sit until they are cool enough to handle. The blistered skins should pull right off with your fingers or a knife. Remove the seeds and finely mince the jalapeños. Place them in a small bowl along with the olive oil and salt and let sit at least 20 minutes to infuse the oil.

When the oil is infused, whisk the vinegar, sugar, and honey into the oil and jalapeños. Start with the minimum amount of sugar and honey, then taste to see if you need more. The amount you need will depend on how hot the jalapeños are. You can set the jalapeño vinaigrette aside, covered, on the kitchen counter for several hours.

To prepare the salads, place 4 watermelon cubes on each of 4 salad plates. Sprinkle the cubes with a few grains of fleur de sel. Sprinkle 1 heaping tablespoon of feta over the cubes on each plate, then top each serving with about 2 teaspoons of the vinaigrette. Serve immediately.

John's Great Greek Burger

My friend John Demos in Raleigh, North Carolina, is a master griller who has worked for years to create what he considers the perfect summer burger. I feel honored that he has shared the recipe with me. The flavors reflect his Greek heritage. And he believes it's impossible to have too much oregano—Greek oregano, of course, if you can find it.

MAKES ABOUT 8 BURGERS

2 pounds ground beef (see Note)
6 ounces crumbled feta cheese
$\frac{1}{2}$ onion, grated
1 tablespoon chopped parsley
2 slices of bread, toasted, crusts removed,
    and finely crumbled
Black pepper to taste
2 tablespoons oregano
Garlic salt to taste (see Note)
1 tablespoon Worcestershire sauce
2 tablespoons olive oil
2 tablespoons lemon juice, plus more for
    brushing the burgers
Buns and burger toppings

Use your hands to mix the ground beef, feta, onion, parsley, crumbled bread, pepper, oregano, garlic salt, Worcestershire sauce, and olive oil and 2 tablespoons lemon juice together in a large bowl. Mold the burgers, making sure each one gets an equal amount of feta. For a juicier burger, make the patties a bit thick and with a smaller circumference instead of making them wide and flat.

Prepare a gas or charcoal grill for cooking. Brush the burgers with a little lemon juice and grill to your preferred doneness, turning once. Brush the burgers with more lemon juice when you turn them and when you remove them from the grill.

Serve with buns and your favorite burger toppings.

NOTE ✹ For the ground beef, John uses 1 pound of 93% lean and 1 pound of 80% lean. Go light on the garlic salt because the feta is salty; you might consider garlic powder (without salt) instead.

Black Bean Summer Salad

This salad saved a summer meal I prepared for a motley crew of vegetarians, vegans, people with dairy sensitivities, and confirmed carnivores. Everyone loved it. It has a place on the picnic table as either a side dish or a light main dish, and it's easily doubled.

MAKES 8 SIDE DISH SERVINGS
OR 4 MAIN DISH SERVINGS

2 cups fresh corn kernels (see Note)
2 (15-ounce) cans black beans, rinsed and well drained
5 or 6 green onions, white and green parts, chopped
1 large sweet banana pepper, seeded and chopped
1½ cups halved cherry tomatoes
6 tablespoons olive oil
2 tablespoons lime juice
2½ tablespoons red wine vinegar
1 teaspoon chili powder
Salt and black pepper to taste
⅓ cup chopped cilantro leaves

In a large bowl, toss together the corn, black beans, green onions, banana pepper, and cherry tomatoes.

In a small bowl, whisk together the olive oil, lime juice, vinegar, chili powder, salt, and pepper. Pour the dressing over the vegetables and toss to coat them. Stir in the cilantro. Refrigerate for at least 1 hour or as many as 3 hours to let the flavors come together.

NOTE ❋ You can use thawed frozen corn but drain it well and lightly sauté it in a couple of teaspoons of olive oil before adding it to the salad. This removes moisture that may make the salad too watery.

Watermelon Lemonade

This cool drink is easy to make and could become a sorbet or frozen popsicles for the kids (pour it into paper cups or popsicle molds and freeze). I use frozen pure lemon juice to make the preparation even simpler. You could really surprise the gang by using a yellow-fleshed watermelon instead of a red one.

MAKES ABOUT 10 SERVINGS

1 small ("personal size") seedless watermelon
1 cup fresh lemon juice
1 cup sugar
5 mint sprigs

Remove the rind from the watermelon and discard it. Chop the flesh into cubes and purée it in batches in a blender. Strain the watermelon juice through a fine-mesh strainer to remove any remaining pulp. Discard the pulp. You should have about 4 cups of juice.

Put the watermelon juice in a pitcher and stir in the lemon juice. Stir in the sugar until it dissolves. Roll the mint sprigs between your hands to crush them and drop them into the pitcher.

Refrigerate the juice for several hours, until thoroughly chilled. Remove the mint sprigs before serving over ice in tall glasses.

Fall

THANKSGIVING FEASTS AND ETHNIC FOOD CELEBRATIONS MAKE THE SEASON GLOW

Food festivals celebrate the region's varied ethnic heritage. And Thanksgiving brings back all those beloved traditional dishes.

Greek Festival

MID-OCTOBER, RALEIGH, NORTH CAROLINA

When I moved to Raleigh in the early 1980s, I had a hard time finding even a bit of baklava. Only three days out of the year could I get Greek food made right: during the Greek Festival, where the food takeout line was double the size of the line to enter and sit down to eat, see Greek dances, and hear Greek music.

Members of Raleigh's Holy Trinity Greek Orthodox Church have been preparing all the festival food for more than thirty years. Local church groups sponsor many other Greek festivals that dot the South.

The Greek presence in the South goes back to the late 1700s, when immigrants arrived in Florida to work on plantations, then fanned out from there. The first Greek Orthodox church in the country was founded in New Orleans.

Many immigrants opened diners and coffee shops. Restaurants were easy entry points for unskilled workers who spoke limited English, and the Greek diner took hold in southern towns. As food writer Kathleen Purvis wrote in the *Charlotte Observer*: "There was a time when Charlotte's restaurant world was firmly Greek-owned. Italian restaurants were Greek, diners and coffee shops were Greek. Barbecue restaurants had baklava on the menu and Parthenon pictures on the wall."

Greek Chicken

There are as many ways to make this dish as there are cooks, but some version of it shows up in most Greek American households. Some people marinate the chicken overnight; others pop it in the oven right away. I got the foundation of this recipe from an usher at a basketball game who got it when he worked as a waiter in a Greek diner. If you can find Greek oregano, use it; the flavor and fragrance, sweeter than Italian oregano, make a difference.

MAKES 6 SERVINGS

½ cup olive oil

¼ cup chicken broth

½ cup lemon juice

2 tablespoons Greek oregano

½ teaspoon salt

½ teaspoon black pepper

3 garlic cloves, chopped

6 pieces chicken, bone-in (use quarters or breasts; thighs are good but double the amount; do not use boneless chicken)

6 medium-sized yellow potatoes, such as Yukon Gold

In a small bowl, whisk together the olive oil, chicken broth, lemon juice, Greek oregano, salt, and pepper until combined. Stir in the garlic. Place the chicken in a large bowl and pour the mixture over it, covering all the pieces. Let sit for 30 minutes to 1 hour.

Cut the potatoes into wedges (no need to peel them). Sprinkle lightly with salt and pepper.

Preheat the oven to 375°. Remove the chicken from the marinade and place the pieces in a single layer in a large, shallow roasting pan. Arrange the potatoes around the chicken pieces. Pour in about 1 cup of the marinade or enough to just coat the bottom of the pan. You may not need all of it; discard the remaining marinade. Roast, uncovered, for about 1 hour or until the chicken is completely cooked through and golden and the potatoes are browned.

Loukoumades

I knew about the wonderful Greek filo-based desserts but had never tasted this favorite until I smelled the aroma of frying dough at Raleigh's Greek Festival. Made on the spot, these Greek doughnuts are soft, crunchy, and sweet all at once. This recipe is adapted from a cookbook produced by the Greek Orthodox Ladies Philoptochos Society in Charleston, South Carolina.

MAKES ABOUT 4 DOZEN LOUKOUMADES

FOR THE LOUKOUMADES

1 (¼-ounce) package active dry yeast
3½ cups sifted flour
1¼ teaspoons salt
2 large eggs
¾ cup lukewarm milk
4 tablespoons sugar
2 teaspoons vanilla
About 6 cups vegetable oil
Cinnamon and chopped walnuts

FOR THE SYRUP

2 cups sugar
5 tablespoons honey

In a small bowl, dissolve the yeast in ½ cup warm water and let sit until it foams. In a medium bowl, stir together the flour and salt.

In a large bowl, beat the eggs until light and fluffy. Add the milk, sugar, and vanilla. Stir in the yeast, then add half of the flour-salt mixture. Beat until smooth. Add the remaining flour-salt mixture, then beat until well blended. Grease a large bowl, add the dough, cover with a lint-free tea towel, and let stand in a warm, draft-free place until the dough is doubled in size, about 1½–2 hours.

Meanwhile, make the syrup. In a large saucepan, combine the sugar and 1 cup water. Bring to a boil, stirring, and boil until the mixture thickens slightly. Remove from the heat and stir in the honey.

When ready to cook the doughnuts, place the vegetable oil in a deep Dutch oven or deep-fat fryer and heat to 370°. Use an instant-read thermometer to monitor the temperature. Drop the batter by scant teaspoonfuls into the hot oil. Cook until golden brown, remove with a slotted spoon, and let drain on paper towels for a minute or so. Stir together the cinnamon and walnuts in a small bowl. While the doughnuts are still warm, drizzle with syrup and roll in cinnamon and walnuts.

Shalom Y'all Jewish Food Festival

FOURTH SUNDAY IN OCTOBER, SAVANNAH, GEORGIA

How many matzoh balls does it take to have a Jewish food festival? "We made 1,200 in all," Harriet Levine told me as she filled bowls at the chicken soup booth. "I made 217 of them myself."

There are more than thirty different food items at the festival, which marked its twenty-fifth year in 2013. That makes it one of the oldest of several Jewish food festivals in the South, including one in Asheville, North Carolina, called Hard Lox.

Where to start? The aroma from Sephardic grilled lamb, stuffed in pitas, was enticing. And I'd never had an egg cream before (they contain neither egg nor cream, but chocolate syrup and seltzer).

This would be a marathon eating afternoon, even with a break at the "Ask a Bubbe" booth, where a genuine Jewish grandmother would answer all my questions about life.

Members of Savannah's Congregation Mickve Israel, the third oldest Jewish congregation in the country, prepare the food. Members become good friends at "challah parties" and other cooking sessions.

Because Savannah loves its canines, there was also a booth selling homemade dog biscuits. I don't know if they were kosher. I should've asked Bubbe.

Food Fest Blintzes

At the festival, cooks heat these brunch favorites in small nonstick electric frying pans and serve them with jam or sour cream. This recipe is adapted from one in the Shalom Y'all Cookbook *from Congregation Mickve Israel in Savannah, Georgia. The original recipe used small-curd cottage cheese in the filling, but my tester felt that farmer's cheese gave a smoother result. If you can't find farmer's cheese, you could substitute cottage cheese, but the filling may not have the same texture. You can easily double this recipe. And a touch of finely chopped fruit in the filling would be a nice variation.*

MAKES ABOUT 12 BLINTZES

FOR THE CREPES
¾ cup flour
½ teaspoon salt
1 teaspoon baking powder
2 tablespoons confectioners' sugar
2 large eggs
⅔ cup milk
½ teaspoon vanilla

FOR THE FILLING
8 ounces farmer's cheese
4 ounces cream cheese or neufchatel cheese
1 tablespoon unsalted butter, melted
1 tablespoon sugar
1½ teaspoons vanilla
½–1 teaspoon salt (optional, depending on whether the
   farmer's cheese is unsalted)
1 large egg

Vegetable oil
Jam and confectioners' sugar

To make the crepes, sift the flour, salt, baking powder, and confectioners' sugar together and place in a blender. Add the eggs, milk, vanilla, and ⅓ cup water and blend until lightly frothy. (Alternately, whisk the dry ingredients together in a medium bowl, then add the wet ingredients and beat well until smooth.) Cover and chill for at least 1 hour or up to overnight.

To cook, brush a 6-inch nonstick skillet lightly with vegetable oil or spray with nonstick cooking spray and place over medium heat. When the pan is hot, lift it from the heat and pour in 3 tablespoons of the batter. Tip the pan quickly to fully coat the bottom evenly. Return the pan to the heat. As soon as small bubbles appear and the edges of the crepe begin to brown, loosen the edges and slide a thin, flat spatula under the crepe. In one movement, flip it over. Brown the second side. When done, remove the crepe to a baking sheet lined with parchment paper or wax paper and let cool.

Repeat with the remaining batter. Place parchment paper or wax paper between the crepes as you stack them.

To make the filling, combine the cheeses, butter, sugar, vanilla, and salt (if needed) in a medium bowl. In a small bowl, lightly beat the egg. Stir 2 tablespoons of the beaten egg into the cheese mixture. Beat ½ teaspoon water into the remaining egg.

Stir the cheese mixture until smooth. Press a layer of plastic wrap on the surface to prevent a skin from forming on top and refrigerate for at least 30 minutes or up to overnight.

To prepare the blintzes, place the chilled cheese mixture and crepes on a work surface. With the more browned side of a crepe facing up, imagine a horizontal line about ⅓ of the way down the crepe. Place a scant 2 tablespoons of the filling on that line and gently tap it into a log shape. (A small cookie scoop is good for this.) Tuck in the sides of the crepe and fold down the top flap to enclose the filling. Then gently roll to form the blintz. Dab a bit of the egg wash along the seam to seal. Place seam-side down on a plate covered with parchment or wax paper.

Repeat with the remaining filling and crepes. Cover loosely with plastic wrap and refrigerate for at least 15 minutes.

To cook, place a 12-inch nonstick skillet on medium-high heat and add about 4 tablespoons of vegetable oil. When the oil shimmers, arrange 4–5 blintzes in the pan, seam-side down. Do not crowd the pan. When the blintzes are lightly golden, turn and cook the other sides until golden.

Serve immediately with jam or a dusting of confectioners' sugar.

NOTE ❋ Don't overfill the crepes. If filling escapes during cooking, it will cause the oil to darken or smoke. If that happens, pour out the spoiled oil, wipe out the pan, and continue with fresh oil. Cooked and cooled blintzes can be frozen. Wrap them individually in wax paper and place in a reclosable plastic bag. Allow the blintzes to thaw overnight in the refrigerator, then reheat in a lightly oiled pan until crisp and warmed through.

Chopped Liver Appetizer Spread

Traditional chopped liver, as the cooks make it for the festival, uses rendered chicken fat known as schmaltz. If you can find it or have the desire to make it, it adds a uniquely rich flavor to this spread. But vegetable oil is a good replacement and easier to find.

MAKES ABOUT 1 ½ CUPS

---

3 tablespoons vegetable oil
½ pound chicken livers, coarsely chopped
1 large onion, chopped
3 large hard-cooked eggs, coarsely chopped
½ teaspoon salt
½ teaspoon black pepper
Crackers or toasted baguette slices

Place a large frying pan over medium heat and add the vegetable oil. Add the chicken livers and onion. Stir and cook, breaking up the chicken livers, until the meat is cooked through and no pink is visible, about 10 minutes. Remove the pan from the heat and let the mixture cool slightly.

Place the chicken liver mixture in a food processor along with the eggs, salt, and pepper. Process in pulses until the ingredients are combined but the mixture still has some texture. Don't overprocess.

Serve with crackers or toasted baguette slices.

ShaLoMein

One of the most popular dishes at the festival isn't traditionally Jewish at all but a Chinese-style favorite. This recipe is adapted from the Shalom Y'all Cookbook *from Congregation Mickve Israel in Savannah, Georgia.*

MAKES 4 GENEROUS SERVINGS

- 1 pound linguini
- 1–2 teaspoons toasted sesame oil, divided
- 1 tablespoon plus 1 teaspoon vegetable oil, divided
- 1 teaspoon chili paste with garlic
- 3 tablespoons soy sauce
- 1 tablespoon hoisin sauce
- ¼ cup sweet kosher wine (such as Manischewitz)
- 2 tablespoons Chinese black vinegar
- 1 tablespoon cornstarch
- 2 garlic cloves, minced
- 1-inch square of peeled ginger, minced
- 1 pound chicken breast, cut into strips
- 20 snow peas
- ½ pound mushrooms, sliced
- 1 bunch green onions, thinly sliced

Cook the linguini according to package directions, drain, and toss with a few drops of sesame oil and 1 teaspoon vegetable oil in a large bowl to prevent sticking.

In a small bowl, mix the chili paste, soy sauce, hoisin sauce, wine, and black vinegar. In another small bowl, dissolve the cornstarch in a small amount of water, enough to make a paste, and stir into the mixture.

Heat a wok over high heat until a drop of water vaporizes on contact. Add 1 tablespoon vegetable oil and swirl to coat the pan. Add the garlic, ginger, and chicken, stirring quickly and vigorously to ensure even cooking. As soon as the chicken is no longer pink, sprinkle in the amount of sesame oil you prefer, then add the snow peas, mushrooms, and green onions. Continue stirring and flipping to make sure the chicken is cooked through and the vegetables are tender-crisp.

Pour the chili paste mixture into the wok, then add the cooked linguini. Use tongs to mix the sauce with the linguini, chicken, and vegetables and simmer until the sauce is slightly reduced and coats the noodles.

NOTE ❋ If you don't have a wok, use the largest frying pan you have and get it very hot. You may have to make the dish in batches if you use a small pan.

Thanksgiving

FOURTH THURSDAY IN NOVEMBER

The Pilgrims get all the press, but the first organized Thanksgiving celebration was actually in the South. When settlers arrived to establish Berkeley Plantation in Virginia in 1619, leaders decreed an annual day of thanksgiving. That was more than a year before the Pilgrims got here. Recently, historians have recognized the Berkeley observance.

Many of today's traditional Thanksgiving dishes originated in the South. Sweet potato casserole is one example. Sweet potatoes are primarily grown in the South. The dish began there and spread around the country as southerners moved.

Many look forward to the side dishes more than the big bird, and everyone has a favorite they must have or it's not really Thanksgiving. That attitude tends to make the meal pretty traditional, but that's OK—it's all about memories.

My must-have is the relish tray. Some people find my obsession with a dish full of pickles odd. But they never saw the colorful bounty of my grandmother's homemade pickled peaches and bread-and-butter pickles, accented by red spiced-apple rings from the store. Now it's my peaches, bread-and-butters, and okra pickles alongside, yes, the apple rings. They must be in the family DNA.

Cajun-Style Rice Dressing

Throughout the rice-growing regions of the South, and especially in Cajun country, rice-based dressings are more common on Thanksgiving tables than the cornbread-and-sage variety. Many contain a lot of meat. For my version, I pared back to chicken livers, which add a delightful earthy flavor, and oysters, because I like oysters in anything.

MAKES 8–10 SERVINGS

4 tablespoons unsalted butter

1 cup chopped onions

1 cup chopped green bell peppers

1½ tablespoons chopped garlic

6–8 chicken livers, chopped

1 pint oysters, drained

1½ teaspoons salt

½ teaspoon black pepper

½ teaspoon cayenne pepper, or more to taste

5 cups cooked white rice

¾ cup coarsely chopped pecans

Place the butter in a large saucepan or Dutch oven over medium heat. Cook the onions, green bell peppers, and garlic, stirring, until soft but not brown, about 5 minutes.

Add the chicken livers and continue to cook until the livers are almost done, then add the oysters. Stir and cook the mixture, cutting the oysters in half as they cook. Make sure the livers and oysters are cooked through.

Stir the salt, black pepper, and cayenne pepper into the mixture, then stir in the rice and pecans. Lower the heat and gently heat through, then serve.

Carol's Sweet Potato Casserole

My husband and I host Thanksgiving dinner, but my sister-in-law, Carol Vatz, always brings the sweet potatoes. She got the original recipe, which is scribbled on the back of an envelope, at a Thanksgiving meal in New York decades ago. She has changed it over the years to reduce the sugar and butter, and I tweaked it a bit more in testing. I suggest starting with the lesser amounts listed, tasting the casserole before baking it, and adding more if you want.

MAKES 6–8 SERVINGS

4 large eggs

1⅓ cups milk

4–8 tablespoons unsalted butter, melted

½–¾ cup brown sugar

4–5 cups mashed sweet potatoes (see Note)

¼–½ cup bourbon

½ cup chopped pecans plus 10–12 pecan halves, divided

½–1 teaspoon cinnamon

½ teaspoon salt

½ teaspoon nutmeg

Preheat the oven to 325°.

In a large bowl, beat the eggs until well combined. Stir in the milk, melted butter, and brown sugar. Add the mashed sweet potatoes and stir until smooth (an electric hand mixer on low/stir is good for this). Stir in the bourbon, chopped pecans, cinnamon, salt, and nutmeg. Taste and adjust the seasoning, if necessary.

Pour the mixture into a well-greased casserole dish and bake uncovered about 45 minutes or until firm. Arrange the pecan halves on the top and put the dish back in the oven for a few minutes to slightly brown the pecans, but don't let them burn.

NOTE ✳ About 5 pounds of sweet potatoes will yield 4–5 cups mashed. I roast rather than boil the sweet potatoes because roasting adds more flavor and less moisture to the casserole. Prick the skins with a fork and roast the sweet potatoes at 375° until the fork passes easily through the flesh.

Aunt Ida's Turkey

I often encourage people to make the effort to record favorite family recipes before they're lost, and this is the recipe I talk about. My husband's Aunt Ida Brody in Kinston, North Carolina, always prepared the Thanksgiving turkey this rather unusual way. It comes out as brown and beautiful as a bird on a magazine cover, with very moist meat. Ida never measured anything, so the family wrangled the recipe from her by standing in the kitchen while she prepared the turkey, asking questions and measuring ingredients before she added them. If cell phones and tablets had existed then, it would have been fun to have a video of that scene.

MAKES ABOUT 10 SERVINGS

1 small (10- to 12-pound) turkey

1 cup cola (see Note)

½ cup orange juice

1 teaspoon onion powder

1 teaspoon garlic powder

Seasoned salt to taste

1 large bay leaf, crumbled

Ample shakes of paprika

1 apple

1 cup chopped onions

1 cup chopped celery, including the leaves

1 cup chopped carrots

Place the turkey in a container with a cover or in a large, heavy cooking bag and pour the cola and orange juice over it. Turn the turkey to cover it with the liquids. Season the turkey all over with the onion powder, garlic powder, seasoned salt, bay leaf, and paprika. Put the apple inside the turkey, then cover the container or securely close the cooking bag. Place the turkey in the refrigerator overnight, turning it occasionally and spooning the liquid over it, especially the breast side.

When ready to cook, spread the onions, celery, and carrots on the bottom of a roasting pan. Add just enough water to cover the vegetables. Remove the turkey from the marinade and place it on a rack above the vegetables in the roasting pan. Discard the marinade.

Preheat the oven to 350°. Cover the turkey with a lid or foil sprayed with nonstick cooking spray. Roast until no pink liquid emerges when the meat is pricked with a fork or an instant-read thermometer registers 180° in the thigh or 165° in the breast. Remove and discard the apple.

Remove the turkey to a serving platter, tent loosely with foil, and let sit for 20 minutes or so before carving. Strain the liquid in the pan to use in making gravy, if you like.

NOTE ❋ Do not use diet or reduced-sugar cola for this recipe. Aunt Ida preferred the cola in the red can. You can also use a whole chicken or a turkey breast instead of a whole turkey.

Mrs. Rozar's Giblet Gravy

Janice Rozar, the mother of my friend Brenda, lives in the little town of Baxley, Georgia, where she grew up. Mrs. Rozar's family expects to see a number of her dishes every Thanksgiving, but her gravy is a must. Giblets are the things in the wrapper that you take out of the turkey before you cook it (unless you forget and your mother-in-law has a fit when she sees you pull it out of the cooked bird). They're usually the heart, neck, gizzards, and liver. I reduced Mrs. Rozar's recipe since I don't cook for thirty like she does. You could double it, adding the giblets from two turkeys or chickens.

MAKES ABOUT 3 CUPS

4 cups chicken broth or water, or some of both
Giblets from the Thanksgiving turkey
1¼ cups chopped onions
¾ cup chopped celery
About ⅛ cup flour
About ⅛ cup cornstarch
Salt and black pepper
2 large hard-cooked eggs, chopped

Bring the broth or water to a boil in a large saucepan, then add the giblets, onions, and celery. Reduce the heat to a low simmer and cook until the giblets are tender, about 1 hour. Remove the giblets from the broth, chop them up, and return them to the pot.

Whisk the flour and cornstarch with a few tablespoons of water in a small bowl to make a smooth paste. Whisk the paste into the gravy and simmer a few more minutes until the gravy is as thick as you like it. You may need more flour or cornstarch to reach the consistency you want.

Taste the gravy and add salt and pepper as needed. Stir in the chopped eggs just before serving.

Apple Pie from the Sisters of Pie

Several years ago, I confessed my fear of making piecrust to a neighbor. She vowed to help me conquer it and invited me to an annual pie-making extravaganza on the day before Thanksgiving. Another neighbor has joined us, and now it's a tradition for we three Sisters of Pie, who occasionally welcome my husband as the men's auxiliary and wine-glass filler. I've learned that making piecrust is one of those things you just have to practice and get the feel for. A pastry cloth and rolling-pin cover help (look for them in kitchen stores; my cloth has helpful 8- and 9-inch rounds printed on it). You can use store-bought crusts, but the flavor of homemade is worth it. Try it once and you'll see.

MAKES 8 SERVINGS

2 cups flour
1¼ teaspoons salt
⅔ cup vegetable shortening
2½ pounds apples (see Note)
½ cup sugar
½ teaspoon cinnamon
¼ teaspoon mace or nutmeg
¼ teaspoon cardamom
2 tablespoons spiced dark rum (see Note)
1 teaspoon vanilla
Milk
1 tablespoon cinnamon sugar

Place several cubes of ice in a small bowl and fill it with water to make the ice water you'll need for the pie dough.

In a large bowl, sift together the flour and salt. Add the shortening. Use a wire pastry blender to cut the shortening into the flour until the mixture looks like it's studded with small peas or like coarse cornmeal. Don't mash the shortening into the flour. Sprinkle a tablespoon of ice water at a time over the mixture and use a spoon to toss it in lightly. Don't mash the dough. You may need up to 4 tablespoons of water, but add one at a time until you have just enough to make a dough that will hold together. You may need less water on a humid or rainy day or more water on a dry one.

Turn the dough out onto a piece of plastic wrap. Through the wrap, lightly massage the dough into a ball, twist the wrap closed, and let the dough sit on the counter for 20 minutes.

Preheat the oven to 425°.

Peel and core the apples and slice them fairly thinly. The food processor is good for this. You should end up with about 5 cups of sliced apples. In a large bowl, toss the apples with the sugar, spices, rum, and vanilla.

Cut off about ⅓ of the pie dough, rewrap it, and set it aside for the top crust. Generously flour a work surface and a rolling pin. Roll the larger piece of dough out smoothly, gently pushing from the center outward in all directions to create a round crust. Don't pound on the dough; roll smoothly. If the edges tear or the circle becomes uneven, simply cut off those portions with a knife and put the pieces back in the center of the dough to re-roll. When the dough is the size of your pie pan, gently work a dough scraper or offset spatula underneath to loosen it from the work surface. Roll the dough over the rolling pin and place it in the pie pan. If the dough tears, simply mash it back together with your fingers.

Pour the apple filling into the crust. It should mound up high but will cook down. Roll out the rest of the dough and place it on top of the filling. Go around the rim of the pan, gently tucking the top crust under the edge of the bottom crust and crimping the edges with your fingers. Use a sharp knife to cut 4 vents in the top crust. Brush the top crust with a little milk and sprinkle on the cinnamon sugar. Place the pie on a rimmed baking sheet to catch any drips.

Bake for 15 minutes, then reduce the temperature to 350° and bake for 40–50 minutes until the crust is brown and juice begins to bubble through the slits. Let the pie cool on a wire rack to room temperature before cutting. The cooled pie may sit, covered in foil, at room temperature overnight before serving.

NOTE ❋ The Sisters feel that a variety of apples offers the best flavor. We use Pink Lady, Winesap, and whatever others look good at the farmers' market. We usually use about 4 different kinds. I make my own spiced rum by adding a couple of sticks of cinnamon, some whole allspice, and a few peppercorns to a bottle of gold rum and letting it steep for 3–4 weeks, but you can purchase spiced rum. If you can't master the crimping for the edges of the top and bottom crusts, just press them together with a fork.

Cranberry-Orange Pie

Thanksgiving is pie day at my house and probably at yours, too. This favorite honors tradition without resorting to that pie made from a giant orange squash. You can use a purchased piecrust, but I strongly suggest you make your own, using the recipe from Apple Pie from the Sisters of Pie (page 105). The lattice top lets the beautiful ruby color of the fruit come through.

MAKES 8 SERVINGS

Pastry for 1 (9-inch) double-crust pie
1 cup sugar
1 (12-ounce) bag fresh cranberries
⅓ cup chopped walnuts or pecans
1 tablespoon flour or cornstarch
½ cup golden raisins
Grated zest of half an orange
1–2 tablespoons Grand Marnier

Preheat the oven to 350°. Line a pie pan with one of the crusts.

In a large bowl, stir together the sugar, cranberries, nuts, flour or cornstarch, raisins, and orange zest. Stir in enough Grand Marnier to moisten the mixture. Pour the filling into the pie pan.

With a pizza cutter, cut the remaining piecrust into approximately 1½- to 2-inch-wide strips. Weave the strips across the top of the filling in a lattice pattern and crimp the edges of the strips where they meet the bottom crust. Place the pie on a rimmed baking sheet to catch any drips. Bake until the filling is bubbly, about 40 minutes.

Sorghum Pecan Pie

Sorghum, a sweet syrup made from a variety of grass, was once widely popular in the South but faded away. Today, it's making a comeback as a hot new ingredient. Sorghum has a milder flavor than molasses, which usually is made from sugarcane. Sorghum is sweeter and more flavorful than corn syrup, the ingredient in traditional pecan pie, which means you need to add less sugar. Pecans are the South's favorite nut, and Georgia has been the nation's top producer since the nineteenth century. In 2013, pecan pie became the official state pie of Texas.

MAKES 8 SERVINGS

Pastry for 1 (9-inch) single-crust pie
1$\frac{1}{2}$ cups pecan halves
3 large eggs
1 cup sorghum
$\frac{1}{2}$ cup brown sugar
1 teaspoon vanilla
2 tablespoons margarine or unsalted butter, melted
Whipped cream

Preheat the oven to 350°. Place the crust in a pie pan and spread the pecans evenly over it.

In a medium bowl, whisk together the eggs, sorghum, brown sugar, and vanilla until the sugar is dissolved. Then whisk in the melted margarine or butter. Pour the sorghum mixture over the pecans.

Bake for 50–60 minutes or until the center of the pie is set. Let the pie cool to room temperature before cutting it. Serve slices with dollops of whipped cream.

Acknowledgments

If I threw a big party for everyone who helped me with this book, it would be an epic celebration that combines every holiday I've written about.

First, I'd like to thank Jill Warren Lucas and Wayne Hill for their help in testing some of the recipes.

For assisting me with historical questions on holidays in the South, I'm grateful to Adrian Miller, Michael W. Twitty, and Jo Ann Williford. The Southern Food and Beverage Museum in New Orleans provided information and some great cocktail recipes. Oral histories compiled by the Southern Foodways Alliance were also a valuable resource.

Organizers of the Blessing of the Fleet celebration in Bayou La Batre, Alabama; the Greek Festival in Raleigh, North Carolina; and the Shalom Y'all Jewish Food Festival in Savannah, Georgia, were generous with their time and recipe information. Judy Walker was an excellent guide to St. Joseph's Day altars in New Orleans. (She's pretty good at catching cabbages tossed from St. Patrick's Day parade floats, too.)

Kind permission to include their recipes came from Stephanie L. Tyson, author of *Well, Shut My Mouth! The Sweet Potatoes Restaurant Cookbook*, published by John F. Blair; Adrian Miller, author of *Soul Food: The Surprising Story of an American Cuisine One Plate at a Time*, published by the University of North Carolina Press; and Elizabeth Wiegand, author of *The Outer Banks Cookbook: Recipes and Traditions from North Carolina's Barrier Islands*, published by Globe Pequot Press. (See you at the next Tar Heels basketball game, Beth.)

Because I've always depended on the patience of others who must listen to my nattering on about recipes, I'm grateful to Kathleen Purvis, Andrea Weigl, and my fellow members of the Association of Food Journalists.

I appreciate the friends and family who were willing to eat experimental recipes and offer informed opinions. They know that just saying "I like this" isn't good enough!

Working with the fantastic staff of the University of North Carolina Press on my second Savor the South book has been a wonderful experience. And there couldn't be a more capable and fun editor than Elaine Maisner. I feel honored to be part of the Savor the South series.

Index

Appetizers and soups
    Apple and Bacon–Stuffed
        Collard Roll-Ups, 27
    Chopped Liver Appetizer
        Spread, 95
    Hop-into-Spring Deviled
        Eggs, 59
    Matzoh Balls, Cajun Style, 54
    Seafood Gumbo, 51
    Sweet Potatoes Restaurant's
        Quick and Easy Hoppin' John
        Soup, 28
    Vietnamese Spring Rolls, 49
Apple and Bacon–Stuffed Collard
    Roll-Ups, 27
Apple Pie from the Sisters of
    Pie, 105
Aunt Ida's Turkey, 102

Black Bean Summer Salad, 82
Blessing of the Fleet, 48–52
    Seafood Gumbo, 51
    Smokin' Mary, 45
Brandy Milk Punch, 35
Breads
    Hot Cross Buns, 62
    Moravian Sugar Cake, 18
    Peanut Butter Muffins with
        Chocolate Drizzle, 24

Café Brûlot, 21
Cajun-Style Rice Dressing, 99
Carol's Sweet Potato Casserole,
    100
Chef & the Farmer's Sugar Baby
    Watermelon Salad with
    Jalapeño Vinaigrette, 78
Chipotle Brisket, 8

Chopped Liver Appetizer
    Spread, 95
Christmas Eve and Christmas Day
    Café Brûlot, 21
    Holiday Coconut Cake, 16
    Lemon-Lavender Jelly, 20
    Martha's Chicken Pie, 12
    Moravian Sugar Cake, 18
    My Favorite Fruitcake, 14
Coconut King Cake, 36
Cranberry-Orange Pie, 108
Creamy Peach Parfaits, 68
Cuccidati, 41

Desserts
    Apple Pie from the Sisters of Pie,
        105
    Coconut King Cake, 36
    Cranberry-Orange Pie, 108
    Creamy Peach Parfaits, 68
    Cuccidati, 41
    Holiday Coconut Cake, 16
    Loukoumades, 89
    My Favorite Fruitcake, 14
    Not Your Grandmother's
        Ambrosia, 23
    Sorghum Pecan Pie, 109
Drinks
    Brandy Milk Punch, 35
    Café Brûlot, 21
    Ginger-Peach Soda, 70
    Rosy Roselle Sipper, 76
    Smokin' Mary, 45
    Watermelon Lemonade, 83

Easter
    Hop-into-Spring Deviled
        Eggs, 59

Hot Cross Buns, 62
Jeanne's Slow-Cooker Country
    Ham, 60
Market Fresh Potato Salad, 64
Entrées
    Aunt Ida's Turkey, 102
    Chipotle Brisket, 8
    Food Fest Blintzes, 92
    Greek Chicken, 87
    How to Do Your Own Oyster
        Roast, 32
    Jeanne's Slow-Cooker Country
        Ham, 60
    John's Great Greek Burger, 80
    Martha's Chicken Pie, 12
    Nanticoke Catfish, 74
    Pasta Milanese with Mudrica, 39
    Seafood Gumbo, 51
    Sephardic Matzoh Lasagna, 56
    ShaLoMein, 96
    Sweet Potatoes Restaurant's
        Quick and Easy Hoppin' John
        Soup, 28
    Very Veggie Brunch Casserole,
        44

Food Fest Blintzes, 92

Ginger-Peach Soda, 70
Greek Chicken, 87
Greek Festival
    Greek Chicken, 87
    Loukoumades, 89

Hanukkah
    Chipotle Brisket, 8
    Sweet Potato Latkes, 10
Holiday Coconut Cake, 16
Hop-into-Spring Deviled Eggs, 59
Hot Cross Buns, 62
How to Do Your Own Oyster
    Roast, 32

Independence Day
    Black Bean Summer Salad, 82
    Chef & the Farmer's Sugar
        Baby Watermelon Salad with
        Jalapeño Vinaigrette, 78
    John's Great Greek Burger, 80
    Watermelon Lemonade, 83

Jeanne's Slow-Cooker Country
    Ham, 60
John's Great Greek Burger, 80
Juneteenth
    Nanticoke Catfish, 74
    Rosy Roselle Sipper, 76
    Smoky Red Rice, 73

Kwanzaa
    Not Your Grandmother's
        Ambrosia, 23
    Peanut Butter Muffins with
        Chocolate Drizzle, 24

Lemon-Lavender Jelly, 20
Loukoumades, 89

March Madness
    Very Veggie Brunch Casserole, 44
    Vietnamese Spring Rolls, 49
Mardi Gras
    Brandy Milk Punch, 35
    Coconut King Cake, 36
Market Fresh Potato Salad, 64
Martha's Chicken Pie, 12
Matzoh Balls, Cajun Style, 54
Moravian Sugar Cake, 18
Mrs. Rozar's Giblet Gravy, 104
My Favorite Fruitcake, 14

Nanticoke Catfish, 74
New Year's Day
    Apple and Bacon–Stuffed
        Collard Roll-Ups, 27

Sweet Potatoes Restaurant's Quick and Easy Hoppin' John Soup, 28
Not Your Grandmother's Ambrosia, 23

Old Christmas
    How to Do Your Own Oyster Roast, 32
    Sassy Cocktail Sauce, 31

Passover
    Matzoh Balls, Cajun Style, 54
    Sephardic Matzoh Lasagna, 56
Pasta Milanese with Mudrica, 39
Peach and Prosciutto Salad, 67
Peach Festival
    Creamy Peach Parfaits, 68
    Ginger-Peach Soda, 70
    Peach and Prosciutto Salad, 67
Peanut Butter Muffins with Chocolate Drizzle, 24

Rosy Roselle Sipper, 76

St. Joseph's Day
    Cuccidati, 41
    Pasta Milanese with Mudrica, 39
Salads
    Black Bean Summer Salad, 82
    Chef & the Farmer's Sugar Baby Watermelon Salad with Jalapeño Vinaigrette, 78
    Market Fresh Potato Salad, 64
    Not Your Grandmother's Ambrosia, 23
    Peach and Prosciutto Salad, 67
Sassy Cocktail Sauce, 31
Seafood Gumbo, 51

Sephardic Matzoh Lasagna, 56
ShaLoMein, 96
Shalom Y'all Jewish Food Festival
    Chopped Liver Appetizer Spread, 95
    Food Fest Blintzes, 92
    ShaLoMein, 96
Side dishes
    Cajun-Style Rice Dressing, 99
    Carol's Sweet Potato Casserole, 100
    Matzoh Balls, Cajun Style, 54
    Not Your Grandmother's Ambrosia, 23
    Smoky Red Rice, 73
    Sweet Potato Latkes, 10
Smokin' Mary, 45
Smoky Red Rice, 73
Sorghum Pecan Pie, 109
Sweet Potatoes Restaurant's Quick and Easy Hoppin' John Soup, 28
Sweet Potato Latkes, 10

Thanksgiving
    Apple Pie from the Sisters of Pie, 105
    Aunt Ida's Turkey, 102
    Cajun-Style Rice Dressing, 99
    Carol's Sweet Potato Casserole, 100
    Cranberry-Orange Pie, 108
    Mrs. Rozar's Giblet Gravy, 104
    Sorghum Pecan Pie, 109

Very Veggie Brunch Casserole, 44
Vietnamese Spring Rolls, 49

Watermelon Lemonade, 83